Memorial Book of the Martyrs of Krasnystaw (Poland)

Translation of
Yisker tsum ondenk fun kdoshey Krasnystaw

Original Book Edited by: A. Shtuntsayger

Originally published in Munich, 1948

A Publication of JewishGen
Edmond J. Safra Plaza, 36 Battery Place, New York, NY 10280
646.494.2972 | info@JewishGen.org | www.jewishgen.org

©JewishGen 2025. All Rights Reserved.
JewishGen is the Genealogical Research Division of the Museum of Jewish Heritage – A Living Memorial to the Holocaust

Memorial Book of the Martyrs of Krasnystaw

Translation of *Yisker tsum ondenk fun kdoshey Krasnystaw*

Copyright © 2025 by JewishGen. All rights reserved.
First Printing: April 2025, Nissan, 5785
Editor of Original Yizkor Book: A. Shtuntsayger
Project Coordinators: Susan and Shawn Dilles
Cover Design: Rachel Kolokoff-Hopper
Layout and Name Indexing: Jonathan Wind

This book may not be reproduced, in whole or in part, including illustrations in any form (beyond that copying permitted by Sections 107 and 108 of the U.S. Copyright Law and except by reviewers for public press), without written permission from the publisher.

JewishGen Press is not responsible for inaccuracies or omissions in the original work and makes no representations regarding the accuracy of this translation.

Library of Congress Control Number (LCCN): 2025933058

ISBN: 978-1-962054-25-6
(Paperback: 190 pages, alk. paper)

About JewishGen.org

JewishGen, is a Genealogical Research Division of the Museum of Jewish Heritage - A Living Memorial to the Holocaust, serves as the global home for Jewish genealogy.

Featuring unparalleled access to 30+ million records, it offers unique search tools, along with opportunities for researchers to connect with others who share similar interests. Award winning resources such as the Family Finder, Discussion Groups, and ViewMate, are relied upon by thousands each day.

In addition, JewishGen's extensive informational, educational and historical offerings, such as the Jewish Communities Database, Yizkor Book translations, InfoFiles, Family Tree of the Jewish People, and KehilaLinks, provide critical insights, first-hand accounts, and context about Jewish communal and familial life throughout the world.

Offered as a free resource, JewishGen.org has facilitated thousands of family connections and success stories, and is currently engaged in an intensive expansion effort that will bring many more records, tools, and resources to its collections.

Please visit https://www.jewishgen.org/ to learn more.

Vice President for JewishGen: Avraham Groll

About the JewishGen Yizkor Book Project

Yizkor Books (Memorial Books) were traditionally written to memorialize the names of departed family and martyrs during holiday services in the synagogue (a practice that still exists in many synagogues today).

Over the centuries, as a result of countless persecutions and horrific atrocities committed against the Jews, Yizkor Books (Sefer Zikaron in Hebrew) were expanded to include more historical information, such as biographical sketches of famous personalities and descriptions of daily town life.

Following the Holocaust, the idea of remembrance and learning took on an urgent and crucial importance. Survivors of the Holocaust sought out other surviving residents of their former towns to memorialize and document the names and way of life of those who were ruthlessly murdered by the Nazis. These remembrances were documented in Yizkor Books, hundreds of which were published in the first decades after the Holocaust.

Most of these books were published privately, or through *Landsmanshaftn* (social organizations comprised of members originating from the same European town or region) that still existed, and were often distributed free of charge. The languages used to document these crucial histories and links to our past were mostly Yiddish and Hebrew. JewishGen has undertaken the sacred responsibility of translating these books into English so that the culture and way of life of these communities will be preserved and transmitted to future generations.

In 1986, a group of farsighted JewishGenners started a project to pool their efforts together in groups based upon their ancestors' towns and donate funds to translate the Yizkor books of their ancestral towns into English. As the translated material became available, it was made accessible for free at https://www.JewishGen.org/Yizkor .

Hardcover copies can be purchased by visiting
https://www.jewishgen.org/Yizkor/ybip.html (see below).

It is our hope that the translation of these books into English (and other languages) will assist the countless Jewish family researchers who are so desperately seeking to forge a connection with their heritage.

Director of JewishGen Yizkor Book Project: Lance Ackerfeld

About JewishGen Press

JewishGen Press (formerly the Yizkor Books-in-Print Project) is the publishing division of JewishGen.org, and provides a venue for the publication of non-fiction books pertaining to Jewish genealogy, history, culture, and heritage.

In addition to the Yizkor Book category, publications in the Other Non-Fiction category include Shoah memoirs and research, genealogical research, collections of genealogical and historical materials, biographies, diaries and letters, studies of Jewish experience and cultural life in the past, academic theses, and other books of interest to the Jewish community.

Please visit https://www.jewishgen.org/Yizkor/ybip.html to learn more.

Director of JewishGen Press: Joel Alpert
Managing Editor - Jessica Feinstein
Publications Manager - Susan Rosin

Notes to the Reader

The images in the original book were reproduced from photographs from the time of the first edition. These reproductions were already of poor quality, being pre-war and at least 30 or more years old. As a result, the images in the book are the best achievable.

To obtain a list of Shoah victims from **Krasnystaw (Poland),** the reader should access the Yad Vashem web site listed below; one can also search for specific family names using family name option. These lists are continually updated by Yad Vashem, so it is worthwhile to periodically search these.

There is more valuable information (including the Pages of Testimony, etc.) available on this website: https://yvng.yadvashem.org/

A list of all books available from JewishGen Press along with prices is available at:
https://www.jewishgen.org/Yizkor/ybip.html

Cover Photo Credits

Cover Design by: Rachel Kolokoff-Hopper

Front Cover:

Illustration of the photo *Krasnystaw town center: City Hall* by Rachel Kolokoff Hopper. [Page 9]

Back Cover:

Illustration of the town of Krasnystaw inspired by a quote from the book: *Krasnystaw was clean and neat. The houses in the center of town were built of stone, painted in light colors. The buildings were one or two stories high; the streets were level, finely paved, and had wide sidewalks. This gave the town a pleasant, cheerful appearance, a quality that was noticed by each stranger.*

The town was considered one of the historic towns of Poland. [page 8]

Back Cover Quote: [Page 7]

Geopolitical Information

Map of Poland showing the location of **Krasnystaw**

Memorial Book of the Martyrs of Krasnystaw

Krasnystaw Geopolitical Information

Krasnystaw, Poland is located at 50°59' N 23°11' E and 128 miles SE of Warszawa

	Town	District	Province	Country
Before WWI (c. 1900):	Krasnystaw	Krasnystaw	Lublin	Russian Empire
Between the wars (c. 1930):	Krasnystaw	Krasnystaw	Lublin	Poland
After WWII (c. 1950):	Krasnystaw			Poland
Today (c. 2000):	Krasnystaw			Poland

Alternate Names for the Town:
Krasnystaw [Pol], Krasnistov [Yid], Krasnystav [Rus], Krasnistav, Krasnostav

Nearby Jewish Communities:

Izbica 7 miles S
Tarnogóra 7 miles SSW
Gorzków 8 miles WSW
Łopiennik Górny 8 miles NW
Rejowiec 8 miles NNE
Kraśniczyn 9 miles ESE
Skierbieszów 12 miles SE
Trawniki 13 miles NW
Biskupice 14 miles NW
Sielec 15 miles ENE
Siedliszcze 15 miles N
Żółkiewka 16 miles WSW
Wojsławice 17 miles ESE
Chłaniów 17 miles SW
Chełm 17 miles NE
Piaski Luterskie 17 miles NW
Zamość 19 miles S

Grabowiec 20 miles ESE
Uchanie 20 miles ESE
Szczebrzeszyn 22 miles SSW
Cyców 22 miles N
Turobin 22 miles WSW
Sawin 22 miles NNE
Wysokie 23 miles WSW
Łęczna 25 miles NW
Zwierzyniec 28 miles SSW
Komarów 28 miles SSE
Chrzanów 28 miles WSW
Bychawa 28 miles W
Świerże 29 miles NE
Głusk 29 miles WNW
Goraj 29 miles SW
Krasnobród 30 miles S

Jewish Population in 1900: 1,763

Project Coordinator Introduction

It is our hope that this translation will help keep the memory of Jewish life in Krasnystaw alive, and perhaps it will add some context to your own family history.

When World War II began, Krasnystaw was a small town with an even smaller Jewish population. However, its location between the larger towns of Chelm, Zamosc and Hrubieszow made this nearly forgotten community witness to events throughout the area.

I chose the words 'nearly forgotten' deliberately. Nearly the entire community was murdered during the Shoah. As with other towns, survivors reconnected after the war ended to write a Yizkor Book in memory of their lost community. They reached out to landsmen who left the town in earlier years for their recollections, and drafted this account. The Krasnystaw Yizkor Book is one of the first, and was edited by A. Shtuntsayger in 1948, while still in a displaced persons camp. The book was published in Munich, Germany using low quality paper, slightly better than newsprint. The high acid content of the paper makes it easily turn yellow and become brittle. Over the last 75 years it appears that relatively few copies have survived.

While many Yizkor books have been digitized - over 650 are available online through a collaboration between the National Yiddish Book Center and the New York Public Library – our online search did not locate any scanned copies of the Krasnystaw book. Remarkably, almost 20 copies turned up in a worldwide search of major research libraries. Two of the copies are at the U.S. Holocaust Memorial Museum in Washington D.C., and we used them to create a scanned copy to support the creation of this volume.

Our involvement in this project started because two of our grandparents came from the nearby town of Hrubieszow. We learned about the JewishGen Yizkor Book translation project in 2019, and jumped at the opportunity to support the effort. In 2020 we volunteered to coordinate translation of the Hrubieszow Yizkor Book. It was amazing to see the translators unlock the previously inaccessible chapters one by one. Each new chapter that was translated helped fill gaps in our family history and provided rich context about the people living in the area and the types of lives they led.

The Hrubieszow book provided an account of the many flavors of Jewish life in the area, and we decided to explore more by translating books from adjacent towns. A Yizkor Book had already been translated for the town of Ustilug, located about 15 miles north east of Hrubieszow on the Ukrainian side of the river Bug. In between Hrubieszow and Ustilug is the town of Horodlo, on the Polish side of the river Bug.

We completed the Horodlo Yizkor Book project in 2024, and Krasnystaw in early 2025. Although the towns are a fraction of the size of Hrubieszow, the variety and intensity of Jewish communal and organizational life described in them is remarkable. The books mention several people and depict some of the same events from different perspectives as they unfold across the area.

The overlapping historical accounts show the value of taking a regional approach to translating Yizkor Books. As a result, we are now working toward translating Yizkor Books for the towns of Dubienka, Skryhiczyn, and Dorohusk located east of Krasnystaw. Next, we hope to translate the Yizkor book for Grabowiec, located south of Krasnystaw between Hrubieszow and Zamosc. Our goal is to translate the Yizkor Books covering the region located south of Chelm and east of Zamosc to the River Bug, which forms the border between Poland and current day Ukraine. The Yizkor book from Chelm has already been translated through JewishGen.

Serving as the translation project coordinator has been rewarding beyond description. We expected to learn about the history and culture of the town, and about the lives and fates of many of its residents. We also hoped to learn new information about relatives that may have been mentioned in the book, and we were not disappointed. A few of the articles were even written by relatives, and others are mentioned in various accounts. These invaluable accounts have enriched our knowledge of our family, and their good deeds are an inspiration.

The translation projects have also brought us into contact with distant relatives and other descendants of town residents, each with their own remarkable stories. Along the way we discovered and joined groups of landsmen from the area that connect online, who have provided support and much appreciated encouragement throughout this project.

We conclude by quoting Max Fire who wrote "I bless the hands of those who, in poring over this book, are honoring the memory of those that we lost."

Susan and Shawn Dilles
April 2025

Acknowledgments

It has been a privilege to help unlock the story of Krasnystaw for new generations of readers. This project was made possible by JewishGen, an organization dedicated to (among other aims) translating more than 800 Yizkor Books from their native languages into English, and making the translations widely available over the internet and through print on demand editions like this one.

We thank Mr. Avraham Groll for his strategic vision, dedication, and oversight of the organization. Mr. Lance Ackerfeld provided expert support and advice for the entire translation effort. His professionalism and extraordinary patience is praiseworthy. We also thank Mr. Joel Alpert, director of JewishGen Press.

We owe the translation itself to Yael Chaver, who also translated the bulk of the Yizkor books for Hrubieszow and the entire Horodlo book. Yael is a uniquely skilled, exceptionally erudite and professional translator. Time and again we were impressed by the research she conducted to clarify obscure words, acronyms, and organization names. Yael 'rescued' the meaning of many words and idiomatic phrases, which may otherwise have been lost.

Thanks go to the hard-working and dedicated team at JewishGen Press team who turned the JewishGen online version of the translation into the book you are holding. The team, led by Susan Rosin includes a graphic artist (to design the cover), layout and formatting specialist, an indexer, a photo extractor, a Library of Congress coordinator, a social media specialist and publicity volunteer. They made the entire process seamless. We just had to review the text a final time.

Finally, we would like to extend our heartfelt appreciation to all of the volunteers that work behind the scenes at JewishGen to help preserve Jewish family history and heritage for future generations.

We were fortunate to have this entire motivated team helping make this translation possible. Their task included working on articles written by different authors with different writing styles and different levels of writing proficiency. As a result, readers may notice these natural stylistic differences.

Translation work is ongoing with dozens of other Yizkor books, and readers may support these ongoing efforts by contributing to the JewishGen general Yizkor Book fund or directly toward specific translation projects.

Susan and Shawn Dilles
April 2025

Dedication

This translation is dedicated to my parents Frank and Evelyn Dilles (z"l), who instilled in us the importance of family, community, and tolerance. Frank served in the U.S. Army in World War II and saw firsthand the impact of the war on Jewish refugees and other victims of the Nazi destruction.

Cars of displaced persons in Germany. The photo was taken by Frank Dilles z"l (the coordinator's father) in 1946 when he served in the U.S. Army during the occupation of Germany in 1945-46.

Photo courtesy of Shawn and Susan Dilles

xvi Memorial Book of the Martyrs of Krasnystaw

Table of Contents

Title Page and Publication Information	Shmuel Zilbershteyn	3
Foreword	Aryeh Shtuntsayger	5
Instead of an Introduction	Ben Zuckerman	6
Krasnystaw (A Monograph)		7

Social Life in Krasnystaw

Political Parties and Organizations	Aryeh Shtuntsayger	13
The "Club"	Aryeh Shtuntsayger	18
The Ahavas-Achim Association	Hershl Zitser	22
Jewish Artisans in Krasnystaw	Aryeh Shtuntsayger	27
Cheders	Aryeh Shtuntsayger	31
Study Houses	Aryeh Shtuntsayger	35

Folk Characters of Krasnystaw

Jewish Wits	Aryeh Shtuntsayger	42
Hassidic Types	Ben Tsukerman	47
Idlers	Yankev Shok	49

Memories

The Jewish Enlightenment	Ben Tsukerman	53
A Few Memories	L. Grinberg	57
The First Emigrants from Krasnystaw in America	Ben Tsukerman	60

Personalities

A Name Enveloped in Sanctity	A. Gelberg	67
Shmuel Mordkhe Zygielbojm (Arthur): A Biography	Y. Sh. Hertz	71
Ben Tsukerman	L. Grinberg	97

The Destruction of Krasnystaw

The Extermination	Aryeh Shtuntsayger	105
In Sacred Memory	Mordechai Futerman	117
My Experiences During the Nazi Regime	Yeshayahu Shtemer	121
List of the Jews Murdered in Krasnystaw		128

Remnants

The Survivors	Aryeh Shtuntsayger	140
My Last Visit to Krasnystaw	Aryeh Shtuntsayger	148
Redress for Jewish Souls	Noyekh Griss	154
List of Surviving Krasnystaw Jews		159
Notes of Thanks		161

Last Name Index — 166

Memorial Book of the Martyrs of Krasnystaw (Poland)

50°59' / 23°11'

Translation of
Yisker tsum ondenk fun kdoshey Krasnystaw

Editor: A. Stunzeiger

Munich 1948

Acknowledgments

Project Coordinator:

Susan and Shawn Dilles

Translated by Yael Chaver unless otherwise noted.

Our sincere appreciation to Yad Vashem for the submission of the necrology for placement on the JewishGen web site.

This is a translation of: *Yisker tsum ondenk fun kdoshey Krasnystaw* (Memorial book of the martyrs of Krasnystaw), Edited by A. Stunzeiger, Munich 1948 (Y 150 pages)

Please contribute to our translation fund to see the translation of this book completed. JewishGen's Translations Fund Donation Form provides a secure way to make donations, either on-line or by mail, to help continue this project. Donations to JewishGen are tax-deductible for U.S. citizens.

Memorial Book of the Martyrs of Krasnystaw

This material is made available by JewishGen, Inc. and the Yizkor Book Project for the purpose of fulfilling our mission of disseminating information about the Holocaust and destroyed Jewish communities. This material may not be copied, sold or bartered without JewishGen, Inc.'s permission. Rights may be reserved by the copyright holder.

JewishGen, Inc. makes no representations regarding the accuracy of the translation. The reader may wish to refer to the original material for verification. JewishGen is not responsible for inaccuracies or omissions in the original work and cannot rewrite or edit the text to correct inaccuracies and/or omissions. Our mission is to produce a translation of the original work and we cannot verify the accuracy of statements or alter facts cited.

Memorial Book of the Martyrs of Krasnystaw

[Page 1]

YIZKOR

Memorial Book of the Martyrs of Krasnystaw

In Memory of the Martyrs of Krasnystaw

Editor: Aryeh Shtuntsayger

Bafrayung Press, Po'alei Tziyon

Munich, 1948

[Page 2]

Title page and illustration by Shmuel Zilbershteyn

Authorization for United Nations Displaced Persons Publication

Authorization No. 241

[Page 3]

This Yizkor Book has been published thanks to the initiative and material support of the chairman of the Krasnystaw Landsmanshaft in Los Angeles, Mr. Ben Zuckerman.

[Page 4]

[Blank page]

[Page 5]

Foreword

Aryeh Shtuntsayger

This Yizkor Book is intended as a modest memorial to our community of Krasnystaw, which was destroyed along with dozens and hundreds of cities and towns in Poland.

The book has no pretensions of being an exhaustive history concerning a Jewish community; rather, it is only a collection of materials written by a few simple Jews, who were lucky enough to survive the vast destruction. Most of the materials are reminiscences that memorialize community life in Krasnystaw during the interwar period.

If survivors reading this Yizkor Book can create their own picture of our town, we believe that we will have achieved our goal.

While gathering the materials, we encountered major problems. First of all, almost everything we received was the product of people's memories. We could not even compile a list of the town's martyrs, because – unfortunately – survivors did not send in the names of murdered friends and acquaintances. We therefore had to be content with noting the names of heads of families, and that, too, from memory alone. It's possible that several families were overlooked. We beg these martyrs to forgive us. May their sacred memory live forever among the Jewish people, together with the memory of the millions of martyrs who left no family members to commemorate them.

* * *

We also express our sincere thanks, in the name of all the Jewish survivors from Krasnystaw, to our distinguished member, Mr. Ben Zukerman of Los Angeles, who was the main force behind the publication of this Yizkor Book. His moral, practical, and material help made possible the appearance of the book.

[Page 6]

Instead of an Introduction

Ben Zuckerman
Chairman of the Krasnystaw *Landsmanshaft* in Los Angeles

We approach the publication of our Yizkor Book with awe.

Doing such serious work is always accompanied by the fear that the commemoration and memorialization of our martyrs, who were so horribly killed by Hitler's murderers, would not succeed.

With bowed heads and trepidation, I beg the forgiveness of our martyrs of Krasnystaw, if we have not properly reflected their terrible suffering and sacred memory in this Yizkor Book. This is because their suffering and torture defies description. Human language has not yet found the proper means of expression.

Great artists have lamented our horrible destruction with sincerity and talent, but they, too, have not yet given voice to the great wailing of the few survivors of the enormous national disaster.

We therefore believe that a simple Jew also has the right to lament and eulogize the innocent martyrs in a colloquial style.

The large monument for the murdered one-third of our nation will probably be erected by an organization that will be set up by the entire nation. But it is our duty to contribute a modest Eternal Lamp, in the form of a Yizkor Book, to commemorate our martyrs, those of Krasnystaw.

[Page 7]

It is our duty to recall the sacred figures of Krasnystaw, who radiated a love for our people, modesty, and sanctity. I would like to mention such laborers as those who lived in the poorest neighborhood of Groblye, and those who lived in the richest neighborhood.[1] In spite of the heavy burden they bore in making a livelihood, they were wonderfully optimistic and were strong in their faith. This gave them the strength and resilience to bear all the torture and persecution that they underwent.

I'd like to embrace the old books, the Talmud volumes bound in boards in the Groblye residents' House of Study, which my great-grandfather Moyshe-Berl built ninety years ago.

We cannot forget our town, which was described so warmly by our classic writers Mendele the Bookseller and Y. L. Peretz.

May this Yizkor Book serve as an eternal memorial candle to remind us of our martyrs. We will always carry their memory in our heart, until we will grant their souls repose in our holy, free land.

Footnote:

1. Groblye is also referred to as Groblie and Grablie. It is a section of Krasnystaw located east of the Wieprz River in the area of modern day Grobla Street.

[Page 8]

Krasnystaw
(A Monograph)

Krasnystaw is the capital of Krasnystaw County in Lublin Province. Although it might seem at first glance that it was a town like all other Polish towns, Krasnystaw had its own features that bestowed a kind of aristocratic character on its residents. This quality was recognized even by the residents of other Jewish towns.

In contrast to the surrounding unkempt towns, such as Izbica, Kraśniczyn, Rejowiecz, and others, Krasnystaw was clean and neat. The houses in the center of town were built of stone, painted in light colors. The buildings were one or two stories high; the streets were level, finely paved, and had wide sidewalks. This gave the town a pleasant, cheerful appearance, a quality that was noticed by each stranger.

The town was considered one of the historic towns of Poland. At one time, under the reign of Kazimierz the Great, there was an aristocratic fortress on the hill.[1] According to local legend, Kazimierz had had a mansion there, where he would come every summer with his Jewish lover Esterke.

By the interwar years, no trace of the fortress remained, except the name of the poor Groblye neighborhood. The name evoked the practice of surrounding medieval Polish towns with an earthen wall, "Groblie" in Polish.[2] It was the poorest part of the town, where the poor lived, Christians as well as Jews.

In ancient times, when Jews were prohibited from living in the town, it was the ghetto where all Jews lived. In more recent times,

[Page 9]

Jews were mixed with Christians, both in the town center and in Groblye.

The Groblye neighborhood was separated from the town by the Wieprz River. This calm river led Noyekh Prylucki to term the residents of Krasnystaw "water-swimmers."[3] In fact, everyone in town could swim. On hot summer days, bearded Hassidic Jews could be seen swimming and diving in the refreshing, warm waters of the Wieprz as though they were – pardon the expression – real sportsmen.

The total population of the town was about 25,000, about 20 percent to whom were Jewish, that is, 5,000. The total, however, included suburbs like the Krakow neighborhood and Zakręcie, in which a few Jews lived. 30-35 percent of the Jewish population lived in Groblie. They constituted the poorest classes, such as shoemakers, tailors, bakers, glaziers, ironsmiths, and wholesale buyers of farm produce.

Over forty percent of the Jews were artisans; the other sixty percents were merchants and retailers. There were also a small number of religious functionaries and people with other occupations.

Krasnystaw town center: City Hall

[Page 10]

Although the overwhelming majority of the Krasnystaw Jews were Orthodox, the town did not give the impression of being backward-looking, unlike many conservative Jewish towns in Poland. There were, however, a few who clung to the old ways and did not follow the new trends. Almost everyone else, even the Hassidic people, allowed modern, worldly life into their homes. This was primarily thanks to the influence of the younger generation, whose members followed different paths.

Religious life was concentrated mainly in the two houses of study: the one in town, which had been newly remodeled after World War I, and the other in Groblie. There were also two small Hassidic synagogues, one of the Turisk sect and the other of the Gora Kalwaria sect.

The older generation was not interested in politics and didn't belong to any political organizations. They did, however, have varied social activities. There was an association of merchants and small shopkeepers, an association of artisans, a mutual aid fund, a peoples' bank, and a burial society.

Social opinions and class differences manifested in the arguments during elections for the city council, the Jewish community leadership, and the House of Study manager. The candidates were mostly opposed by the artisans and the Hassids (who were usually merchants and shopkeepers.) In all cases, the upper hand was that of the poorer class – the artisans. Thus, for example, the town rabbi was supported and elected by the artisans and poorer residents. They also comprised a large proportion of the community council; even the chairman belonged to that class. One might say that the artisan class dominated the town.

As a result, the young people became interested in politics, and had their own political organizations. These included Zionist organizations, the Mizrachi, Agudas-Yisroel, HeChalutz-Po'alei Tziyon, Po'alei Tziyon (Left-wing), and a professional association that was influenced by the extreme left wing.[4]

Almost all the young people of Groblie, with a few exceptions, were members of the Communist professional association, or its sympathizers. The young people of central Krasanystaw mostly belonged to the various Zionist organizations.

The cultural heritage, along with the Peretz Library, was transmitted to the young folks by the first modernizing members of the community: Shlomo Sharf, Leyzer Laufer, and all the others mentioned by Ben Zuckerman in his reminiscences in this book.

[Page 11]

The group that included Ben Zuckerman and other friends were the heralds of the modernizing impetus in Krasnystaw.

The current writer, who was a member of the younger generation and one of those who received their heritage from the older group, later took over the Peretz Library and developed it further. It would be safe to say that the Library was the center of modern culture for the young Jews of the town. It was the focus of their social life. The young people of Groblie, however, were organized in a professional association and had their own library. They did not reach the same cultural level as the others.

The Peretz Library, which was developed by many Zionists and Zionist pioneers (many of whom have survived and live in Israel), merits its own essay.

[Page 12]

[Blank page]

Translator's footnotes:

1. Kazimierz the Great reigned over Poland during 1333-1370.
2. The Polish 'groblie' means earthen embankment or wall.
3. Noyekh Pryłucki (1882–1941) was a Yiddish scholar, journalist, and political leader.
4. Mizrachi, HeChalutz-Po'alei-Tziyon and Po'alei-Tziyon (left-wing) were socialist Zionist organizations. Agudas-Yisro'el was an Orthodox party.

[Page 13]

Social Life in Krasnystaw

[Page 14]

[Blank page]

[Page 15]

Political Parties and Organizations

by Aryeh Shtuntsayger

As is well known, the Jewish towns of Poland had an intensive, lively political and social life. Almost all the political parties of Polish Jews would be represented in every town, regardless of size.

The parties carried on lively ideological arguments, which often became heated. In hindsight, the "heatedness" of the Krasnystaw political debates was pleasantly atypical. Though right-wing, left-wing and centrist parties were all represented, relations were polite. There were hardly any "incidents" stemming from political differences.

It is worth noting that the Bund organization was not represented in our town.[1] There was a lone Bundist, named Knobel. He was a poor, hard-working carpenter, who was rarely out on the street. Everyone knew him, though, because the moment he appeared he would become the center of a group of challengers, and heated discussions would begin. With true Jewish single-mindedness, he would defend the Bundist principle of a "national-cultural autonomy." He was not bothered by the mild ridicule of his antagonists.

There were actually two main political groupings in the town, one Zionist and the other Communist. This followed the division between

[Page 16]

Groblie, where poorer people lived, and the town. The residents of Groblie were inclined towards Communism, whereas the people in the town were mostly Zionists. Of course, not all Groblie dwellers were Communists, just as not all town dwellers were Zionists. These ideological differences were mostly typical of young people. Older people, with a few exceptions, were not interested in such "nonsense."

The Communist-aligned young people gathered around the "Professional Association of Needlework and Similar Crafts." They did not actively campaign against the bourgeoisie, for the simple reason that there were no members of that class in town. The employers for whom the young tailors and carpenters worked were extremely poor themselves, and would have supported a "worldwide Socialist revolution," as they termed it, as long as they could make a living. On the other hand, the Association had considerable funds for organizing the self-education of the youths whose education had been disrupted at the early age of 12 or 14, when they had started working. Thus, their education consisted of one year of secular school, or two years of Talmud Toyre or the cheder.[2] Sometimes they attended two or three years of government school. The Association ran self-education groups, in which people studied in Dr. Elyashev's Folk University. They also read books, newspapers, listened to lectures on political economics, Marxist theory, etc.

In this way, the Association was extremely important for ensuring the cultural standards of the working youth. Its members developed faith in books and in knowledge, which distanced them from the trashy, immoral pleasures characteristic of the young people of other nations. Yet the police authorities considered them dangerous, and often arrested their leaders, especially around May 1. Most of them were distinguished by their great devotion to their ideals, and readiness to serve long prison sentences for their beliefs.

The ruling ideology in "town," as noted, was Zionism. Here, as in Groblie, young people constituted the majority of the organizations. Older youths were mostly observant Hassids, and indifferent to politics.

The unobservant youngsters were all "General Zionists," in other words – Zionist sympathizers, who weren't allied with any particular stream of Zionism. They read the *Haynt* newspaper, contributed to the Keren Kayemet (Jewish National Fund), and voted for Yitskhok Grinboym in elections.[3]

[Page 17]

But the youngsters were organized in HeChaluts and Beitar. Thanks to HeChaluts and HeChaluts HaTsair, many of them received agricultural training, and emigrated to the Land of Israel.

In addition, the older members of HeChaluts initiated various cultural activities. They ran the I. L. Perets Library, the only Yiddish library in town (the association had a different library in Groblie). They also organized a cultural association, known as the Club, where events. Lectures, discussions, and similar activities were held.

This work by the Zionist activists had a great effect on the young people of the town. First, it brought a breath of fresh air into the reactionary, clerical atmosphere in which most young people had grown up. It also forged a Jewish national awareness among those youths who had been educated in a worldly way and tended to become assimilated.

Herzl Academy and "Soldiers' Circle"[4]

Seated: Hersh Vaysvasser, Yidl Shtuntsayger, Moshe Ayzenberg, member of the high command – Avrom Valdman, Shloyme, Pinches Gartler, Leybl Tenenboym.
Seated: Hersh Vaysvasser, Yidl Shtuntsayger, Moshe Ayzenberg, member of the Beitar high command, Moyshe Lusthoyz, Noyekh Vaysvasser, Yoysef Mernshteyn.

[Page 18]

The "Leftist Po'aley-Tsiyon" organization should also be mentioned. Though it barely existed in the last few pre-war years, for quite a few years it had had a positive influence on the youngsters' development of social awareness, but on no other aspect of society in the town.

Generally speaking, the youth were organized by social class. Most young workers belonged to the "Association." Middle-class children and those from moderately well to do homes were aligned with HeChaluts, which was associated with Po'aley-Tsiyon. The children of richer families were usually not organized; it was beneath them to be associated with the "rabble," yet they were incapable of setting up their own organization.

The Revisionist organization was an exception. It consisted of an odd mixture of young people from all social classes, who completely lacked political consciousness.

The older people were also organized, but in associations that were purely professional and non-political. Thus, for example, the artisans had their Artisans' Association, which helped to raise their consciousness as professionals. This association was mainly concerned with organizing help for poor and needy artisans, and with electing delegates to the councils of the community and the town.

There was also a small-business association, which organized a charity fund and a people's bank.

All these organizations were busy and active; but the principle of mutual aid was predominant.

Except for two or three persons who were mainly out for their own ambitions and interests, the leaders, for the most part, worked without expectation of reward. This is especially noteworthy, considering that they were all cut down by the hands of Hitler's murderers.

May their memory be for a blessing.

* * *

Translator's footnotes:

1. The General Jewish Labor Bund in Lithuania, Poland and Russia, generally called The Bund or the Jewish Labor Bund, was a secular Jewish socialist party initially formed in the Russian Empire. The principle of national-cultural autonomy proposed de-territorializing the nation, or organizing ethnic groups into a national unit without having to confine them within geopolitical borders.
2. Boys started studying in the cheder (or khyeder) at age five, and learned Hebrew, prayers, and some Torah. At about age eight, they transferred to a Talmud Toyre and began studying Mishna and Talmud.
3. The General Zionists were a centrist Zionist movement, with views that were largely colored by central European culture. *Haynt* (*Today*) was a Yiddish daily newspaper, published in Warsaw from 1906 until 1939. The Keren Kayemet LeIsrael (Jewish National Fund) was founded in 1901 to buy and develop land in Ottoman Syria (later Mandate Palestine) for Jewish settlement. Yitskhok Grinboym (1879-1970) became the leader of the Zionist Federation of Poland in 1918 and served as a Jewish

representative in the Polish Parliament, the Sejm, in the 1920s. He was a towering figure in Polish Zionism throughout the 1920s.
4. The image caption is duplicated below the image and is garbled. My translation follows the versions as printed.

[Page 19]

The "Club"

by Aryeh Shtuntsayger

"The Club" was the term used by the Jews of Krasnystaw for the building that housed the Y. L. Perets library.[1] In its last years, the library comprised 1,500 books in Yiddish and Hebrew, including classic works by Yiddish writers and translations of the best works of European writers, went through several transformations until it took its final form as the Club.

It was a legacy from the town's first modernizing Haskalah residents.[2] However, as most of those Jews gradually emigrated overseas, while others married and were busy with day-to-day practical issues at the expense of cultural activity, the library's contents were relegated to boxes under the beds of some young people. Eventually, a new group of cultural activists developed, and the library was revived at "Royze's."

The location was known by the name of the elderly Jewish woman who lived there and rented them part of her room; she herself was accommodated in a corner with her bed, curtained off by a white sheet.

Among those who helped to reconstruct the library we should mention the chairman, Mendl Raychman (may his memory be for a blessing). He was extremely energetic, even though he was hunchbacked. Also noteworthy was the secretary, Moyshe Prechter, the son of the town cantor.

The library was very active during that period, mainly among the young men of the Study House.[3] The works of Smolenskin, Mapu, Perets, Mendele the Bookseller, and Sholem-Aleichem guided them along the paths of modern Jewish life.[4]

[Page 20]

Thanks to the library, the Jewish girls of the town received a cultural Jewish education that prevented their assimilation. The library was also the main educator of Zionist youngsters.

The founders of the "Club" and the chief organizers of the HeChaluts and Po'aley-Tsiyon parties in Krasnystaw

Sitting from right to left: Chayim Meir Perlmuter, Yeshayahu Shtemer, Moyshe Blat
Standing: Shloyme Kerpel, Aryeh Shtuntsayger, Meir Zayfer, Meir Dresher, and Gershon Shtern

The library later moved to a different location, which served as the gathering spot for General Zionist youth. Let me also mention the librarian, Hadassa Finkelshteyn (peace be upon her), who was a major contributor to Zionist and cultural activity among girls. This was a continuation of the work begun by Esther Maymon, who had emigrated to Canada.

Others who were active in the library, besides the above-mentioned Mendl Raychman and Moyshe Prechter, were Hadassa Fayershteyn,

Moyshe Drayblat, Shloyme-Shiye Vayser, Yisro'el and Leybl Ayzenberg, Yisro'el Pechter, Leybl Shteyn, and others.

As the group members grew older, they began searching for a new generation to continue their Zionist and cultural work. This was the start of the HeChaluts HaKlali organization. The leader of the latter organization, Gershon Shtern, headed activities among the young people up to the devastation of World War II. Another member was

[Page 21]

Aryeh Shtuntsayger, who became the secretary before the community's devastation. In addition, the following members were also active: Chayim Perlmuter, Yechezkel Shtern, Moyshe Blat, Sheyndl Prechter, Arn Shok, Shloyme Kerpel, Mendl Ayzenberg, Binyomin Shmaragd, Moyshe Raychman, Meir Zayfer, Meir Dresher, Dvoyre Lerer, Borech-Leyb Fayershteyn, and others.

Many members of this group emigrated to the Land of Israel, others to other countries, and some were tragically murdered together with the Jewish community of the town. They constituted the liveliest factor in the Zionist and cultural activities of the young people in the town.

The Buffet at the Club

Right to left: Miriam Yungman, Aryeh Shtuntsayger, Chayim-Meir Perlmuter, Hersh Zilberman, and Lola Perlmuter

The group deserves mention as the motivating force behind the authentic Zionist atmosphere that permeated the younger generation, from 1932 to the beginning of World War II. The war marked the end of the Jewish community in Poland, the Jews of Krasnystaw among them.

* * *

Translator's footnotes:

1. Yitskhok Leyb Perets (1852–1915) was a Yiddish and Hebrew poet, writer, essayist, dramatist, and a major cultural figure.
2. The Jewish Enlightenment movement (Haskalah) was a secular intellectual movement among the Jews of Central and Eastern Europe between 1770 and 1880. It promoted rationalism, liberalism, relativism, and enquiry.
3. The Study House (Bes-Medresh) was a framework for religious study found in almost all Jewish communities. The young male students honed their scholarly abilities by intensive study of the Mishna and Talmud, guided by tutors.
4. Perets Smolenskin (1842–1885), was a popular Enlightenment writer, whose work attracted a wide and enthusiastic readership and influenced the consolidation of a nationalist Haskalah movement and Zionist ideology. Avraham Mapu (1808–1867) was a key figure in the Russian Haskalah movement, and the first Hebrew novelist. Mendele the Bookseller (Mendele Moycher-Sforim, 1808-1867) is the pen name of Sholem Yankev Abramovich, a prolific Hebrew and Yiddish writer. He is considered the founder of modern artistic prose in Hebrew and Yiddish. Sholem-Aleichem was the pen name of Sholem Rabinovich (1859-1916), one of the founding fathers of modern Yiddish literature, and a supreme humorist.

[Page 22]

The Ahavas-Achim Association[1]

by Hershl Zitser

As one of the few surviving Jews of Krasnystaw, I would like to add my contribution to this book memorializing Jewish life in our town. I wish to mention a group of progressive young people, who were organized in the Ahavas Achim association during the last decade before World War II.

The association was founded at the initiative of the murdered members Yisro'el Varman and Avrom Zayfer, and the present writer.

Dark clouds had already begun to threaten the Jews of Poland. Anti-Semitism was spreading in the country and had taken deeper root in

Krasnystaw than in many other places. This was because there weren't many Jews in the town; they constituted only about 10-12 percent of the population. For the same reason, the Jews were poorly represented in the communal institutions, and the anti-Semites had free rein to do as they pleased. Extreme reactionary ideology, with its extreme Jew-hatred, was well known in the area. It's worth noting that whereas there remained a small Jewish population in the neighboring towns until the second half of 1943, Krasnystaw was Judenrein as early as the first half of 1942.[2]

In the prewar years, the head of the town's tax department, Drozdowski, was famous in the area as a sadistic Jew-hater. Due to the tax collectors,

[Page 23]

many of the Jewish small-business owners were ruined. Young people were especially hard-hit, as they had just begun their professional lives as shopkeepers or artisans. This was one of the reasons that impelled young people to organize mutual aid societies to help themselves.

Any political organizing was impossible, as the group included members of political parties; the majority were Zionists. Besides, worries about livelihood dampened the political ardor of many. Some of the members became politically indifferent. As Ahavas Achim was non-political, members of all political stripes could join, on the basis of friendliness and mutual aid. Discussions were quite sophisticated, yet never caused amicable relations to unravel, and they continued to exist to the end.

Ahavas Achim often held parties and meetings on Shabbat and holidays, so that members could enjoy themselves in familiar surroundings. The association numbered about one hundred members.

Memorial Book of the Martyrs of Krasnystaw

The following members were murdered, with all the Jews of Krasnystaw:

Yisro'el Varman and wife	Sholem Singer
Avrom Zayfer and wife	Yosi Schneider and wife
Yisro'el Fechter and wife	Dovid Pelts and wife
Bentshe Rozenblat and wife	Shmuel Fleshler and wife
Leybl Shteyn and wife	Mendl Binder and wife
Shloyme Yehoshua Vayser and wife	Dovid Zilbertson and wife
Betsalel Hofman and wife	Shloyme Zilberlicht and wife
Avrom Fecher and wife	Motl Fishler and wife
Borech Yoyneh Perlmuter and wife	Moyshe Dreksler and wife
Shmuel Perlmuter and wife	Mendl Raychman and wife
Yehoshua Zitser and wife	Yehoshua Tsuker and wife
Dovid Boymfeld and wife	Moyshe Kerpel and wife
Itshe Blat and wife	Moyshe Lusthoyz and wife
Moyshe Drayblat and wife	Mechl Lerman and wife
Zaynvl Mitlman and wife	Yitskhok Tsuker and wife
Yissocher Rozenblat and wife	Simche Boym and wife
Borech Hersh Luft and wife	Motl Fayershteyn and wife
Yoysef Mernshteyn and wife	Yisro'el Ayzenberg and wife

[Page 24]

The following association members were lucky enough to survive, without their families:

> Hershl Zitser
> Leyzer Kornfeld
> Yitskhok Bergerman

> Arn Lerner
> Berl Buchbinder
> Borech Hartshteyn

The following members happened to survive with their families:

> Moyshe Raychman
> Mendl Rozentsvayg

> Asher Shok
> Yisro'el Perlmutter

The Ahavas Achim association created a mutual aid fund, which offered members in financial difficulties an interest-free loan. There was also an "advice committee," whose mission was to provide advice or legal aid to members. The association also had an internal tribunal which mediated disputes between members and often dealt with business disputes as well.

The association elected Avrom Zayfer and Dovid Boymfeld to the community council, and Sholem Zinger – to the town council. These delegates were supported by a wide circle of people outside the association as well.

It is also worth mentioning the frequent meetings between various members. The atmosphere was warm and friendly. People used to meet mostly at the homes of Yisro'el Varman or Avrom Zayfer, to have pleasant conversations on cultural matters.

My heart shatters when I remember the beloved, dedicated members, bright souls, and devoted friends, and their connections with each other.

I particularly want to mention the Judenstaat devotee Bentshe Rozenblat, and his ongoing discussions with the left-wing Yehoshua Vayser, conversations that were quite sophisticated.[3] I would also like to mention my close friends Borech Yoyne Perlmuter and Yisro'el Fechter, who were pure, perfect souls.

Bentshe Rozenblat in particular suffered at the beginning of the German occupation, as he worked with other representatives of the Jewish community. At that time, people still believed that the Jews could pay off their destroyers and ease the plight of the town's Jews.

[Page 25]

I'd like to mention one incident of German sadism and the emotional suffering that Bentshe underwent. It was in December, 1939. One night, around midnight, when my wife, children, and I were asleep, there was a hurried knocking at the door. We woke up in fear, knowing that Germans stood outside. Terrified, I opened the door. Two SS officers and two German soldiers came in, leading Bentshe. Our friend, as pale as death, wanted to say something, but was unable to utter a word as he saw the fear in the eyes of my wife and children. My wife gave him a glass of water, to refresh him.

The SS officer began yelling at him, "Jew! Speak! If not, you'll be shot immediately!"

With great effort, Bentshe turned to me and said, "Mr. Zitser, you must come to the barracks first thing tomorrow morning and bring all the money. Otherwise, you'll be shot."

Apparently, Bentshe had to go from one Jewish house to another, to convey the order. When the Germans left, we breathed more easily, having survived, but extremely fearful. However, we were devastated by the fact that Bentshe, of all people, had to be the one who was forced to bring the German extortion order to the town's Jews.

The Ahavas Achim association did everything it could to bind its members as a group. They founded their own synagogue, where our members Borech-Yoyne Perlmuter, Betsalel Hofman, and others starred as fine cantors. We enjoyed the wonderful religious melodies and folk songs that Yisro'el Fechter sang. Even Hassids often came to hear the beautiful services led by our "cantors."

And the Hitlerite beasts, may they be cursed for eternity, aided by Poles and Ukrainians, cut down our intimate, happy circle of friends.

We mourn for those who have been lost and are no longer with us.

Translator's footnotes:

1. Ahavas Achim (or Ahavat Achim) means "brotherly love."
2. Judenrein ("cleansed of Jews") was the Nazi term for a town where all Jews had been expelled or murdered.
3. Theodor Herzl began advocating for a Jewish state as the political solution for both anti-Semitism and a Jewish secular identity in his pamphlet *Der Judenstaat*, published in Vienna in 1896. Herzl is considered the founder of modern political Zionism.

[Page 26]

Jewish Artisans in Krasnystaw

by Aryeh Shtuntsayger

Jews are often accused of being a nation of merchants and middlemen, who hate to work. But Krasnystaw provided clear evidence that Jews like to work and can be exceptional workers and artisans.

Forty percent of the Jewish population of Krasnystaw was occupied with manual labor and artisanship. The overwhelming majority of Krasnystaw's Jews were occupied with tailoring, shoemaking, smithing, harness making, upholstery, carpentry, painting, and other crafts. Jews also did other, less complex jobs, such as water-carrying, cart-driving, mill work, and manufacturing (at Fecher's furniture factory). In addition, there were shop clerks, accountants, and the like.

Thus, the majority of Krasnystaw's Jews lived honest, hardworking lives. Naturally, most were very poor and barely made a living.

Regardless of their difficult situations, these Jews made sure to provide for their spiritual needs. The poor neighborhood – the Groblie – had its own study house.[1] The older artisans were organized in an artisans' association, whereas the working youth had their professional association. The older generation was less advanced and incapable of improving their economic conditions by applying modern methods. But in their own way, they fought for their rights and democratic opportunities.

The "battle" was often a bit comical. Thus, for example, they

[Page 27]

quibbled over recitation of the Book of Jonah, the haftoreh for Yom Kippur, or recitation of a blessing before a particularly prestigious Torah reading, or a finer hakofeh during Simchat Torah, to make sure these pious practices fall to an unlearned or poor Jew.[2] The poor artisans even had their own rabbi, the so-called Turbiner Hasidic Rabbi.[3] I remember once asking a coachman, who happened to be not very observant, why he needed a rabbi. He answered me in plain language, "Those fools [also] need a rabbi – don't we? We, too, need a rabbi." The logic may sound a bit comical, but it is based in the attempt to be equal – spiritually, at least – to the "respectable Jews" who "have a rabbi of their own."

Shmuel Zaltsman at his shoemaking bench with his daughter, in Krasnystaw

The artisans' association began its activities with the goal of improving the economic conditions of the artisans, through mutual aid. It fought, in an organized manner, for its own representation in the councils of the community and the town. An artisan did not want the aid of the "respectable Jews,"

[Page 28]

but wanted to have someone familiar with whom he could speak freely and who would help him in various matters.

I would like to mention two artisans of outstanding simplicity, honesty, and unusual solidarity with the organized artisans' association: Shloyme-Yehoshua Vayser and Yoyneh Mandltort.

Shloyme-Yehoshua Vayser was a painter by trade, a poor man who was always hard at work, very capable, innately intelligent, and a fine scribe. He was the secretary of the workers' association, who had never sought a position in the community council but always had time to help a friend in need. He did so whole-heartedly, without pettiness. He helped people who needed to submit an official request, at no charge, and aided association members with no thought of compensation, always unassuming, in a good mood, never giving himself airs.[4]

Yoyneh Mandltort was a community medical practitioner, who considered himself better off than other artisans. He was the president of the artisans' association. Yoyneh healed poor, sick children and adults, never thinking about charging them a fee. He would often go of his own volition to visit a sick person who was poor.

The poor trusted him more than they would a physician. Although he considered himself an intellectual, he was not proud and was on familiar terms with every single working person. He was quiet and decent, and no one had a bad word to say about him.

These two people, whose souls were pure, had much sympathy for another's suffering. Let these few lines be their monument. They were brutally murdered by the German killers, together with the entire Jewish population of Krasnystaw.

May God avenge their blood.

Most of the artisans' children worked alongside their parents or learned a different profession from another artisan. Only the few artisans who were financially better off allowed their children to study.

These young people organized themselves in a professional association of Needle Workers and Allied Professions, which actually included all the young workers.

The middle classes and shopkeepers looked down on artisans, so that working young people were almost completely disconnected from other "middle-class" young people. The working youth had

[Page 29]

profound self-respect. They were politically aware, left leaning, and anxious to learn. With very limited means, often at the expense of food, they created their own library, organized self-education groups, and did much to raise the cultural level of the working youths. The young people lived under difficult conditions, and did not have many friends. They dreamed about a better future and believed in it. The horrendous murderers cut down most of their young lives. Only a few survived, by fleeing to the U.S.S.R.[5]

We honor their holy memory!

Translator's footnotes:

1. The Hebrew term for 'Study House' and 'House of Study' is Beit Midrash.
2. The haftoreh is a selection from one of the biblical books of the Prophets, read in synagogue immediately following the Torah reading on Shabbat and holidays. Chanting the haftoreh for Yom Kippur, which largely consists of the book of Jonah, is prestigious, and brings with it the promise of wealth. People often pledged sums of money to the synagogue for the chance to recite one of these selections or blessings. A hakofeh is one of the circuits (at least seven) that an honored worshiper walks around the synagogue hall on Simchat Torah, carrying a Torah scroll past the congregation. Simchat Torah is the holiday that marks the completion of the previous year's Torah reading cycle and the start of the new year's reading cycle.
3. The Rabbi of nearby Turobin was known as a leader of artisans, who would travel to various Jewish communities.
4. The expression "never giving himself airs" refers to not making himself seem important or acting superior to the person he was helping.
5. U.S.S.R. is the Union of Soviet Socialist Republics, or Soviet Union.

[Page 30]

Cheders

by Aryeh Shtuntsayger

Like all other towns in Poland, Krasnystaw had many cheders with various melameds.[1] The youngest boys were taught by a particular kind of melamed, who taught Hebrew to beginning students until they were capable of reading the Torah. The next oldest group taught Torah with Rashi's commentary; these children also began to study Talmud, starting with rules about basic damages.[2] Finally, Talmud teachers worked with the older students, teaching them Talmud and commentaries. Students who were interested in studying to become rabbis also learned some *Yoreh De'ah*.[3]

The local professional melameds mostly taught the youngest boys, and some taught Torah with Rashi. The Talmud teachers were largely recruited from among poor scholars whose business had collapsed, or an amateur teacher who needed extra income.

The two major melameds of young children were Reb Moyshe Melamed in the Groblie neighborhood, and Reb Leyzer Melamed in the town.[4] The latter also taught in the Talmud Torah, where the poorest boys studied.[5] They studied free of charge. That cheder was managed by the two administrators, Ben-Tziyon Halpern and Yehoshu'a Vizenberg.

The present writer studied with almost all the melameds in town: Reb Moyshe, and even Reb Motele, a teacher who enjoyed pinching the young children, and usually harassed the poorest of them. I also studied with Reb Hersh "Messiah," as well as with the town's expert in Jewish law, and with a number of amateur melameds. My brightest memory, however, is of Reb Moyshe, with whom I took my first steps toward literacy at the age of four or five.

[Page 31]

He was a quiet man, not elderly, with a pale, gaunt face, a black beard, and a pair of kind, slightly faded eyes, which expressed a strange suffering and irritation. I remember that years later, while I was attending the Polish school, I thought that the picture of Christ wearing the crown of thorns, which hung on the wall above the head of the teacher, had a very strong resemblance to Reb Moyshe. My heart always beat more strongly every time I made this "heretical" comparison. However, I could not ignore it. It even made Christ less frightening and revolting, contrary to the usual reaction of every Jewish child who entered a Polish school.

Reb Moyshe was not the stereotypical irritable melamed. He was kind-hearted, and rarely hit a student. He lived in the tumbledown house that belonged to Leyzer, the cemetery attendant, in Groblie. In summer, children used to play in the courtyard or next to the wall of the cheder, near the dusty, muddy Groblie road, where the puddles rarely dried up.[6] Reb Moyshe summoned the children inside in pairs. After the children would call out the syllable *G-gu! D-du! R-ru!* and so on through the alphabet for ten or fifteen minutes, Reb Moyshe would release them back into the courtyard and summon another pair. In the winter, the children sat along the long bench at the wall, playing with matchsticks or jacks. The melamed's wife, a quiet woman, whose voice was never heard, busied herself at the rough kitchen with "coffee" and cooking potatoes for her husband. She asked the children to help only when she needed to strain the hot potatoes. She would hold the boiling-hot pot in both hands, and the children would run to open the door so that she could run into the corridor with the steaming pot.

The children especially enjoyed "nighttime" school. After Hanukah, the children who were more advanced and were studying Torah with Yiddish translation would start attending cheder at night. In the evening, they would learn more advanced Torah portions. For these occasions, they would make their own lanterns, as follows. First, they broke off the bottom of a bottle and used it as a holder for half a shoe-polish tin, in which they placed a candle. They then attached a string and used it to light their way to cheder and back. The cheder was cozy during those evenings. They sat around a table with a kerosene lamp that cast yellowish light, and the teacher chanted as he taught the wonderful winter portions from the Book of Exodus.

The cheder of Reb Leyzer Melamed in town was not much different.

[Page 32]

Like Reb Moyshe, he lived in a broken-down shack, on the street of the butchers.[7] The single room was also full of children and tumultuous. But Reb Leyzer was older, gray-bearded, and gruff, who never set down the disciplinary whip. His status was because almost all the wealthier people in town (some of them now quite old) had studied with him as children. He had begun teaching as a young man, and taught continuously for decades, into his old age. He died at over seventy years old, while teaching at his table: he put down his tired, grayish-white head on the prayer book, and fell asleep like a small child, dying peacefully. When his students saw that he was asleep, they went out to play in the courtyard. It was evening before the neighbors noticed that Reb Leyzer had fallen asleep forever.

Reb Hersh the Talmud teacher was quite different. No one knew why he was called Hersh "Messiah." He was middle-aged, thin, with a shortish black beard. Reb Hersh was one of the "modern" melameds and well versed in the Bible. He taught his students sections from the Bible, in addition to Talmud.[8] Because of his Bible teaching, he was considered a heretic by the Hasidic Jews of the town. However, his emphasis on the Bible led all his students to become fervent Lovers of Zion and devoted settlers in the Land of Israel.[9] Reb Hersh died young, from lung disease. His two sons, Moyshe and Leyzer, live in a kibbutz in Israel.

These melameds were joined by a few "semi-official" melameds who taught children. Noteworthy among them was Reb Yekele Shtern, a very honest, smart man, a merchant who had become impoverished and was now supported by the earnings of his sons, Gershon and Yechezkel, and his daughter Broche. However, so as not to be considered a freeloader, he taught a few of the "better" students. Reb Avromtshe Meir Varshniter had a soda-water stall. As business was very bad, he also taught three or four good students – not for the money, supposedly, but because it was a mitzvah. Another was Reb Mendl, expert on Jewish Law, an elderly, observant person without a livelihood, who also taught a few rich young men.

The present writer studied with all the above-mentioned melameds.

Now, when all that was Jewish in Krasnystaw has been eradicated by the Hitlerite beast, as happened in many Polish cities and towns, the sacred figures of these quiet, sincere Jews surface in my memory. They

[Page 33]

lived modest, impoverished lives, and believed in the mission of planting seeds of Jewish morality in the hearts of their students. They lived almost like ascetics, denying themselves worldly pleasures, eating dry bread crusts on weekdays, and offal on Shabbat so as to eat some meat.

These are the people whom Hitler blamed for provoking the war. The benches of the cheders were the breeding-grounds for "warmongers" such as Artur Zygielbojm, who freely gave his life in protest against the war and the murders. Their blood cries out from the earth and boils, like the blood shed by the prophet Zechariah, which calls out for revenge.[10]

Let these few lines be a monument to their sacred souls, and to their bodies, that were not buried according to Jewish law.

May their souls be bound up in the bundle of the living.

Translator's footnotes:

1. Cheder, or kheyder (literally "room") is the singular for the elementary education of young boys up to about age 8. The term may refer to the class itself or to the place where it is held. The teachers were called melameds (literally "teachers").
2. Rashi (the acronym for Rabbi Shlomo Yitzchaki, 1040-1105) was a French rabbi who wrote comprehensive commentaries on the Talmud and the Hebrew Bible in plain language, which was accessible to the youngest readers. His commentaries are in wide use to this day.
3. *Yoreh De'ah* is a compilation of Halacha (Jewish law) by Rabbi Jacob Ben Asher in about 1300. It is the most diversified area of Jewish law and served as the basis for later books of Halacha, notably Rabbi Yosef Karo's *Shulchan Aruch* (1563).
4. Reb is a common honorific, which was always used for a Jewish teacher. The term should not be confused with the title Rabbi.
5. A Talmud Torah is a school for boys who had outgrown cheder. The students are taught Torah, Talmud, and some Halacha.
6. Cheder studies usually took place in the home of the teacher.

7. The text does not specify whether the butcher's houses and/or shops were located on this street.
8. The Bible per se was not taught in this type of traditional Jewish education, which placed more emphasis on the Talmud.
9. The proto-Zionist "Lovers of Zion" organizations were established in 1881¬-1882 with the aim of furthering Jewish settlement, particularly agricultural settlement, in the Land of Israel. In Hebrew they are known as "Hovevei Zion" or "Hibbat Zion".
10. Artur (Shmuel) Zygielbojm (1895-1943) was the leader of the Jewish socialist Bund in interwar Poland. "The blood of Zechariah" is a reference to Matthew 23:34-36.

[Page 34]

Study Houses

by Aryeh Shtuntsayger

The Jewish community of Krasnystaw was not large; it numbered about four hundred families. However, there were quite a few houses of prayer in the town, besides two study houses. The "large" study house, as it was known, was in the town, whereas the other – as its name indicated – was in the Groblie district. There were also several small Hasidic synagogues and places where minyans would gather to pray.[1]

The large study house was a beautiful brick building that had been built long before World War I. It, along with most of the town's structures, was destroyed in that war, and restored during the 1920s.

The study house in a small town was not only a place to hold prayers but also a community center, where observant, old-fashioned Jews maintained their social life. Saturday afternoons were the time for an itinerant preacher's sermon, and the location of daily discussions before evening prayers which focused on politics as well as on ordinary social and town matters. It was the site of meetings to discuss repairs to the ritual bath [mikvah], the burial society [Chevra Kadisha], or the synagogue manager and, in later years, to hold Zionist meetings about the Keren Kayemet and Keren HaYesod Palestine settlement funds. Naturally, that was where the social yearnings of ordinary Jews played out, yearnings for higher social standing, a prayer spot at the eastern wall, leading a prestigious prayer on Shabbat, and other social honors. Each and every Jew was interested in the study house.

During the first postwar years, when the large study house had been reduced to a ruin, many Jews had to pray in the Groblie study house; it was owned by the poorer groups of artisans, most of whom lived in Groblie. Others prayed in the Turisk study house, and it was this group

[Page 35]

that began to restore the large study house. As money was scarce, they held a meeting and decided to sell permanent seats, for men and women (the latter prayed in the women's section).

The same "class warfare" as in the original study house played out in this meeting as well. At that time, more well-off artisans lived in the town center than in Groblie. They resolved not to give up the entire eastern wall to the wealthier Jews.[2]

The large study house in central Krasnystaw

Image taken in 1947, when the study house was turned into a grain barn by the Gentile agricultural cooperative

The issue led to blows, and the artisan "revolutionaries" won. The synagogue manager, Moyshe Levkovich, was chosen from among the ordinary Jews. The wealthy Jews wanted to build themselves a new synagogue, so that they wouldn't have to pray in Groblie together with tailors and cobblers, but the "poor souls" were vanquished by the ordinary folks.

The Turisk Hassids, who considered themselves "aristocrats,"

[Page 36]

gathered in their small synagogue. This was a partially destroyed building in a side street, near "Leyzer's Stream," so called because it was near the cheder of Leyzer Melamed. This synagogue was also where young unmarried scholars spent their evenings studying Talmud and playing pranks on each other between immersing themselves in Talmudic discussions. They would wave towels around, while secretly inserting a piece of paper under someone's collar and setting it on fire. They were so noisy that eventually Refoyl, the shammes (who lived in the damp, neglected cellar of a partly ruined house), would come in and put an end to the "rascals'" rampaging.[3] The boys were deathly afraid of him. Luckily for them, Refoyl the shammes was extremely nearsighted, and missing one lens of his exceptionally thick eyeglasses. Thanks to that, the "rascals" managed to slip out of his grasp and run away. The bolder among them would play a trick on him by crawling under a bench next to him, knowing that he would not notice.

He was not hated, because Refoyl the shammes was a good-natured man who liked to joke – he often sat and chatted with the study house group – and because of his male goat.

Refoyl owned a male goat, which could not be slaughtered.[4] It ran around freely and became friendly with the cheder children and the boys in the study house and synagogue. It was known as "Refoyl's Billy goat." As it was familiar with the cheder students, it grew bolder and often walked into the small synagogue through its open door, to the amusement of the students.

Studying in the small synagogue was lively and happy. The students could play freely in the adjoining square, without fearing Gentile boys. In the summer they could also spend hours bathing in "Leyzer's Stream."

Yet once the large study house was rebuilt, the boys moved there; it was far larger, cleaner, and enjoyed fresh air. During the last years before World War II, the numbers of study-house boys decreased. There was no future in religious studies. Many became "spoiled," and learned a trade, or left for Warsaw to settle down. In the long winter evenings, the study house was populated by only a few elderly men who warmed themselves on the oven-bench or near the Torah-reading stand.[5] The most common conversation topic was about the old days, when the "Jap" fought against "Ivan."[6]

[Page 37]

The Groblie study house was usually empty. The sons of artisans' families had to start working at an early age and learn a trade or help their fathers. In the evenings, it was the refuge of the town's homeless people: Ayzikl, a clumsy, half-insane man who could eat endlessly without becoming full, and "crazy Henekh," a cast-off youth, who was in the habit

Memorial Book of the Martyrs of Krasnystaw

of constantly washing his hands in the nearby "Zhikl" brook near the study house.

But all the houses of prayer were full and lively on Shabbat and holidays. There were often arguments about performing the more prestigious readings, such as the Jonah haftoreh for Yom Kippur, or the blessing before the annual beginning of Torah reading, on Simchat Torah. Even among the artisans who prayed in the Groblie synagogue there were more important and less important members.

A regular minyan of followers of the Ger Hassidic group also assembled at the slaughterer's house.[7] One of their characteristics was the fact that they would break for an hour or two on Shabbat and holidays between the morning service and the additional Musaf service and devote the time to studying.

The Zionist minyan was founded by about twenty progressive young men, Zionists, who had never been very observant. They were uninterested in praying, but as sons-in-law of observant parents, or simply wishing to appear well to do, and having nowhere to be on Saturdays, "when all the Jews go to pray," established their own minyan. One of them, a young man named Betzalel, a brilliant student from a nearby town, had married a local girl. He considered himself a fine musician and really wanted to lead the prayers. He would be set at the reading stand to serve as a cantor, while the others would read the *Haynt* newspaper or carry on discussions about Zionism.[8]

The terrible Nazi executioners destroyed the pleasant lives of small-town Jews. Almost none of the young people survived; they were horribly murdered. The location of the Groblie study house is now a vegetable garden cultivated by Gentiles. The Turisk small synagogue is occupied by a Gentile, and the sweet voices of small Jewish boys are no longer heard from the cheder of Leyzer Melamed. These innocent Jewish children were taken to Belzec, where they were hideously murdered. The town's large study hall is once again broken down and abandoned, and its windows are blocked by wooden boards; it serves as a grain barn for the Gentile agricultural cooperative.

In the last days of the war, the present writer took a risk and visited all these sites. The scene of the abandoned sites was nightmarish. These abandoned sites were where Jewish life quivered and breathed, and from which so many were horribly uprooted,

[Page 38]

among them many near and dear Jewish fathers, mothers, and small children.

Is it possible to set down on paper the piercing pain one feels at a moment like this? The pain will never subside and will forever demand revenge for the innocent blood that was spilled.

These desolate spaces are left with another curse: may the blood of these martyrs sear the earth and serve as a reminder that the murderous, beastly perpetrators are cursed forever.

Translator's footnotes:

1. A minyan is a group of ten men, the quorum required for traditional Jewish communal worship.
2. The eastern wall of a European synagogue, which faces Jerusalem, is the most prestigious area for seating.
3. The Shammes maintains a synagogue and its religious articles.
4. According to Jewish law, a first-born male goat should be offered to God as a tithe and may not be slaughtered and consumed.
5. The eastern European masonry oven was usually located in the center of the house and retained its heat for a long time. It served many purposes, including warming people on a built-in bench.
6. This refers to the Russo-Japanese war (1904-1905).
7. The 'slaughterer' refers to the Shochet, or ritual slaughterer. They were familiar with the details of the Jewish laws governing the kosher slaughter and preparation of meat.
8. The *Haynt* ("Today") was the premier Yiddish newspaper in Poland and appeared daily in Warsaw during 1908-1939.

[Page 39]

Folk Characters of Krasnystaw

[Page 40]

[Blank page]

[Page 41]

Jewish Wits

by Aryeh Shtuntsayger

Authentic Jewish jokes and aphorisms were developed by ordinary Jewish folks. The cleverness of Jewish humor has been recognized even by non-Jewish scholars and students of the field.

Each Jewish town had its wits and aphorists, who came from unsophisticated settings. Unfortunately, large portions of original folklore and jokes have been lost. The YIVO institute, in Vilnius, laid special emphasis on collecting Jewish folk sayings, jokes, proverbs, and the like. But the ever-productive ocean of Yiddish folk wisdom had not been exhausted before the destruction of the YIVO archives and its collections, which erased a large part of these riches.[1]

Krasnystaw, too, had its share of Jewish wits and intellectuals who produced aphorisms. The most popular of them was Leyzer Foyglfus (known as Leyzer, Avrom's son), Refoyl Rosentsvayg – a young man known as Fintshele – Aron Tsuker, and Arn Oksenberg (Arn, Bere's son).

Leyzer, Avrom's son, was the town's gravedigger, and a person who had lost his previous livelihood. He was quiet and dejected, extremely poor, yet someone who never passed up a chance to tell a joke or say a proverb, and was always at ease. He took the "material" for his jokes from his "profession" and his poverty. Prime occasions for his jokes came up during the mornings of the High Holidays, as well as when he downed a brandy on Simchat Torah and Purim, or during a Kiddush[2]. Some of his aphorisms and jokes are worth presenting here.

[Page 42]

Leyzer would earn a few pennies every time a Jewish woman visited the cemetery to mark the anniversary of a death. He would lead her to the grave of her father or mother. Every year, a rich woman would come from Warsaw, to visit the grave of her father, who was buried in Krasnystaw. She had not erected a headstone, and Leyzer showed her the spot every year. However, he never went to the trouble of finding the precise location. Wherever he happened to stand would be designated as the grave she was seeking: "He's buried here!" The next year, he would stop at a different location and point it out: "He's buried right here!" But the woman remembered something from the previous year's experience, and asked him, "Didn't you show me a different spot last year?" Leyzer didn't lose his calm, and said, "Have you always lived in the same place? Well, your father also moved, and he's living here now…"

In front of his dilapidated, dumpy little house, stood a mound of chopped timber, compressed into bales. One day, he was sitting on the mound and resting, when an acquaintance passed by.

"Moyshe, come here. I'm inviting you to the 'ball'," motioning to the mound he was on.

On Purim, Leyzer performed his own version of the Passover "Four Questions." The first question was, "Why is my roof crouching over my house, yet I have no eggs?" The second one was, "Why has my wife let her mouth run free, yet I have no goose fat?" The third was, "When there's a hole in your shoe, why does the water leak in, but when there's a hole in a pot, why does the water leak out?" And finally, "What should I do if I find a crumb in the pot, which could be a grain that's forbidden on Passover?"

On Simchat Torah, Leyzer would present "sermons" that he invented, such as the following.[3] "In the Talmud, the sage Rav says, "With regard to one who betroths a woman with a loan, i.e., he previously lent this woman money and he now says that she is betrothed to him by means of that loan, she is not betrothed."[4] According to this decision, Rav was a mean person who stood in the way of betrothals. But as it happens, we know that Rav was kind, because the verse states, "O Lord, pardon my guilt, for it is great." This answer can be countered by an allegory. Once there were two friends, Yoyneh and Shloyme. Yoyneh borrowed money from Shloyme, which caused Shloyme to go to prison. The townspeople said that Yoyneh had landed Shloyme in hot water. When people heard this, they came to Shloyme's house for Kiddush on Shabbat. Shloyme, however, had no brandy, as he didn't think guests would be coming, and was very sad. As it happened, Rav was also there,

[Page 43]

and proclaimed, "He who betroths a woman by means of a loan has not carried out a betrothal and therefore does not need to offer a Kiddush." Thus, we can see that Rav was really kind – he took pity on Shloyme..."

One more witticism at the expense of his own poverty:

Leyzer, Avrom's son, who, incidentally, was quite short, was out on the street, met an acquaintance, and complained that his situation was difficult, and that he had no money. His friend advised him to borrow a few złotys. Leyzer retorted, "Who'd loan me money? After all, I'm a very small earner." (This is a pun on his own name: he wouldn't be able to make enough money to return the loan.)[5]

Arn Oksenberg, known as Bere's son, was just as poor as Leyzer. He lived his entire life in the cellar of a house owned by a rich non-Jew. The first floor, above him, was occupied by a non-Jewish lawyer, Fiechowitz. In spite of his poverty, Arn was always in good spirits and made fun of his poverty. This is one of his jokes.

Arn met a "progressive" young man, and challenged him: "Your modern ideology is not worth a penny, and is definitely wrong."

"Why???"

"Your Copernicus explained that the earth turns on its axis. That's impossible and couldn't possibly happen."

"Why?"

Memorial Book of the Martyrs of Krasnystaw

"If the earth turned on its axis, sometimes I would be on the top, and Fiechowitz would be on the bottom. But for years now, I've always been on the bottom (in the cellar) and Fiechowitz has been on top (on the first floor)."

Refoyl Rozentsvayg was the Shammes [Sexton] of the Turisk synagogue and also made some money with his little cart and its tottering little horse, which he would hire out to anyone in town who needed to haul something. As far as jokes are concerned, he always competed with Leyzer. Every time they met, they would test each other's wit. Once, Refoyl met Leyzer with mock anger: "You're burying the whole town!" referring to his grave-digging job.

Leyzer immediately gave as good as he got: "Are you any better? You're turning the whole town topsy-turvy!" referring to his cart driving and haulage.

Fintshele was considered an idler. His wife supplied their livelihood. He almost always sat in the study house, but rarely

[Page 44]

sat and studied. He was smart and liked to debate whomever he could. He also never missed a chance to outsmart his opponent with a clever joke.

One Krasnystaw Jew, who was newly rich, was called Moyshe Ringworm[6]. He wanted to convince everyone that he was a Talmudic scholar by posing trick questions in the study house. As Moyshe sat there house one day with a volume of Mishna, he challenged Fintshele with one of these questions.

"Look, Fintshele. The Mishna says that the evening recitation of Shema Yisrael can be done once the stars are visible.[7] Actually, it doesn't make sense. Why does the Mishna need to tell us when to say the evening Shema? Don't I already know that we say the Shema in the evening?"

Fintshele looks serious and says, "You understand, of course, that you wouldn't know if the Mishna hadn't said that. Moyshe, I'm really surprised that you should ask such a question. On the other hand, though, you've got something else on your brain," meaning ringworm on the scalp.

Hershl Tsuker was a different kind of joker. He was wealthy and was considered very smart. He liked to emphasize life's paradoxes, and to state truisms in an amusing way. Here is one of his gems.

"What is the meaning of the biblical phrase 'And they received from one another, and said Holy'?"

"If one receives (money) from another, the giver can say kaddish for it".[8]

These were the jokes of simple folks. I'd like to say a few serious words about them, not only because this article is part of a Yizkor book that is a blood-saturated document about atrocities unprecedented in the history of mankind, but because the present writer is profoundly convinced that this was the case. These people lived a hard, but decent, life. Their figures shine in my memory, as well as the figures of dozens more of Krasnystaw residents. They were all hard workers, whose pleasures were very few. Regardless of their poverty, however, their moral stature was great. They could not imagine living otherwise than as Jews. And it was as Jews that they were murdered.

Their memory will be sacred to our future generations.

* * *

Translator's footnotes:

1. The Yiddish Scientific Institute, established in 1925 in Vilnius, is an organization that preserves, studies, and teaches the cultural history of Jewish life throughout Eastern Europe, Germany, and Russia as well as orthography, lexicography, and other studies related to Yiddish. It relocated to New York at the beginning of World War II, and is the pre-eminent research center for Yiddish studies today.
2. Kiddush is Hebrew for 'sanctification'. It is a blessing recited over wine or grape juice to sanctify the Shabbat and Jewish holidays. Additionally, the word refers to a small repast held on Shabbat or festival mornings after the prayer services and before the meal.

3. Such folk humor is deeply rooted in the tradition and discourse of Talmud study as well as in everyday life.
4. The garbled quote is from Kiddushin, 6b, the Mishna tractate that deals with family law. The speaker in the original is the sage Abayeh (though there is an important sage known as Rav); the substitution is part of Leyzer's performance. The reasoning for the invalidness of the betrothal stems from the prohibition of drawing interest on loans. Betrothals are as binding as marriage. Leyzer's "commentary" is rich in puns on the language of prayer and rituals; for instance, the second quote (Psalms 25:11) contains the Hebrew word for "great," which is transliterated as "rav."
5. Leyzer, the diminutive of Eliezer, means 'earner' in Yiddish.
6. The Yiddish word 'parkh' means both 'bastard' and 'ringworm'
7. Shema Yisrael, from Deuteronomy 4, is a prayer that serves as the centerpiece of the morning and evening prayer. It opens with an affirmation of the monotheistic essence of Judaism. It is traditional for Jews to say the Shema as their last words, and for parents to teach their children to say it before they go to sleep at night.
8. This is a pun on a quote from the Targum Jonathan, an ancient Aramaic translation of the Bible created in the Land of Israel. The quote is from the translation of Isaiah 6:3 "They [the angels] said, Holy" (kadosh). The Aramaic for the Hebrew kadosh is Kaddish, the name of a prayer said when mourning a deceased person. The implication is that the loan is as good as dead, i.e., will never be repaid.

[Page 45]

Hassidic Types

by Ben Tsukerman, Los Angeles

Shabbat and holidays in Krasnystaw were truly elevated by a pleasant, sacred atmosphere, and a devoutness that reigned in all the Jewish homes and synagogues as well as in the study house. The Hassidim shone in their long satin coats, fur hats, and clothing made of silk and velvet. The poverty-stricken faces had shed their cares, and now radiated joy.

Is there anyone who doesn't remember the dignity of the Jews, who were transformed into royalty during Shabbat and holidays?

Is there anyone among the natives of Krasnystaw who doesn't remember the classes in Torah and Rashi's commentary that Pinkhes, Yeshaya's son, taught to the tailors and shoemakers, those who gulped down every word and every thought?[1] Who doesn't recall the festive meal that Fayvl, the synagogue janitor, would offer in the old study house to mark the end of Shabbat? It did not offer delicacies, but the Bnei Heicholo' song and the tidbits of learning that were offered in the late afternoon lifted the participants to a higher plane of being.[2]

I remember the Shabbat evening celebration at the home of Mekhl, the rabbi's son, who was very poor. He had never dealt with money but spent all his time studying Talmud. He was ordained as a rabbi but could not make a living at it. His energetic wife, Chane, had the yeast concession. Aided by her grown daughters, who were of marriageable age, she barely made enough money to survive. But that did not prevent them from holding the festive Shabbat meal with great enthusiasm in the attic that was their home.

[Page 46]

In 1920, when I visited Poland and my home town of Krasnystaw, there was little left of the pleasant old-time idyllic life. The first German salvo obliterated many of the material and spiritual properties and sent them up in smoke. I encountered skepticism and pessimism everywhere. However, when I went to the ruin that had once been the Turisk synagogue, I found Gershon, the glazier's son (may he rest in peace), who was continuing to study Talmud. He was one of the last Mohicans in Krasnystaw.[3]

One Shabbat day, as I was riding the train, I met a Jew and his daughter. The long-bearded Jew admitted that until recently he had been a firm believer in Judaism. As I looked at him, I remembered the Jews that I had known in my childhood. They were all devout believers, who were ready to sacrifice themselves for the sake of Jews and Judaism. How far removed this Jew, who was desecrating Shabbat, was from characters like the Gur Hassid Ts. B. Gershon Mayman, or the Turisk Hassid Yisro'el Lerman, who would shake the walls of the study house with his fervent Shema Yisro'el. Even unlearned, but profoundly honest types such as Chayim Yehuda the peddler, and Motele the water-carrier, who was constantly reciting Psalms, or my father, Yehoshua Tsukerman (may he rest in peace), would never relinquish a speck of their faith, let alone desecrate Shabbat in public.

These were Jews with high moral characters, and souls that were as transparent as crystal.

"It is a pity about those who are gone and are no longer among us."[4]

Translator's footnotes:

1. Rashi (acronym of Rabbi Shlomo Yitzchaki, 1040-1105) was a French rabbi who wrote comprehensive commentaries on the Bible and the Talmud. These commentaries are popular and widely studied to this day. Tailors and shoemakers were considered lower class and unlearned.
2. "Bnei Heicholo" (Sons of the Palace) is a mystical song, popular in Hassidic groups, that is attributed to Rabbi Yitzchak Luria, author of the *Kabbala*.
3. Note: The writer is inserting an internationally popular trope. The expression means that Gershon was the last of his kind in that time and place. It refers to the title of the historical novel "The Last of the Mohicans" by James Fennimore Cooper. The book has been one of the most popular English-language novels since its publication and has been adapted numerous times and in many languages.
4. This phrase is common in a eulogy.

[Page 47]

Idlers

by Yankev Shok

Who did not know a man by the name of Ayzik? Everyone knew him. He was a character worth describing.

When people wanted to disparage someone, they would call that person Ayzik. For example, anyone eating voraciously would be described as "gobbling it up like Ayzik." A way to embarrass someone would be to call him "as smart as Ayzik."

Ayzik was physically powerful, strongly built, but his great fault was laziness. He never wanted to hear of work and earning money. As if that weren't enough, he had an insatiable appetite and was never satisfied. If someone asked him, "Ayzik, why don't you work and make some money?" he would answer, smiling like a simpleton, "God almighty didn't create work for Jews. The prayer says 'You have chosen us from all peoples,' and we are, after all, the chosen people. Why should I work? Besides, how can a Jew work? Saturday is Shabbat; on Mondays we read the Torah portion. Tuesday, as everyone knows, is market day in Krasnystaw, and you have to spend the whole day there. Wednesday is for recovering from the market. Thursday comes along, and we need to read another Torah portion. Friday isn't worth discussing – it's the eve of Shabbat. I ask you – does a Jew have time to work? Secondly, why should I work? For example, when it rains, I take refuge in the 'bottle-woman's' house where I can shelter, just like people who have houses.[1] And as far as food is concerned, don't we have middle-class people

[Page 48]

who make big pots of cholent[2] for Shabbat? And how am I different from all the other Jews? I go to Chayim Lorber's house, like many others."

And that's what happened. When Ayzik came over on Shabbat and sat on the steps, Volf's wife was the first to see him, and let the others known that Ayzik had arrived. And do you know who else was staying there? Shloyme Hersh the leather merchant, Shloyme Mushkat, Moyshe Shiye, Beynish the grain merchant, Moyshe Chayim the bookbinder, Mendl Shmuel Shmaragd, Shaul Liberman the tailor, Rachmil the glazier, his son Shmuel, and others.

Just imagine: every homeowner prepared cholent, knowing that Ayzik had to eat his fill on Shabbat. After the meal, they would ask Ayzik whether he was full, and he would answer, "What do you mean, full? I will only be really full when the Messiah comes. When that happens, pasta and beans will rain down from the sky. The whole Turisk synagogue will be the pot, and the lectern will serve as a ladle. That's when I'll be full."

Believe me, Ayzik was not the fool he was made out to be. He would sometimes utter an aphorism. For example, he once came to Chayim Lorber's house, who was known to be wealthy. He owned houses and barracks, and married into the family of the Hasidic leader of Turisk. Zaynvele Klepfish was also related to him by marriage. Not everyone could enter Chayim Lorber's house. But Ayzik could come in freely, and the host enjoyed Ayzik's witticisms.

One Friday, Ayzik walked into Chayim's house and went through all the rooms until he came to the dining room, when Chayim was lying on the couch. Chayim did not notice Ayzik immediately. Ayzik, on the other hand, looked around the room and noticed the table, which was ready for Shabbat with twelve loaves of challah, a carafe of wine, and a platter of fish. When Chayim noticed Ayzik standing by the door and looking in, he asked, "What would you like to say, Ayzik?" Ayzik responded, "What can I say, Chayim? Everyone says that Ayzik is a fool. I ask you, Chayim, if everything on the table – challahs, fish, and wine – would be in Ayzik's house, wouldn't Ayzik be the one lying on the couch? So, is Ayzik really the fool and Chayim the clever one?"

Yet Ayzik the idler never caused anyone harm.

Why did Hitler's beasts murder him?

* * *

Translator's footnotes:

1. The reference is not clear.
2. Cholent is a traditional slow-simmering Sabbath stew in Jewish cuisine.

[Page 49]

Memories

[Page 50]

[Blank page]

[Page 51]

The Jewish Enlightenment[1]

by Ben Tsukerman, Los Angeles

Let me start by saying that this memoir will not be a complete survey, but rather the humble memories of an ordinary Jew. I begin with the period of the Russo-Japanese war.

Our town was in turmoil at the time. The Jews were divided in two groups: pro-Japan and pro-Russia. The old study house was an open forum, where heated debates took place. The information for these debates was taken from the Hebrew newspaper *HaTsfira*, which was published in Warsaw under the editorship of Chayim Zelig Slonimski (may he rest in peace), as well as the Yiddish *Der Fraynd*, published in St. Petersburg and edited by Asher Ginzburg.[2] True, there were not many readers of either publication. But the "heavenly" Enlightenment, as it was sometimes known, had begun to have an effect on the town, and forbidden publications were secretly making the rounds. These included Avraham Mapu's Hebrew *Ahavat Tziyon* and *Ashmat Shomron*, Peretz Smolenskin's *HaTo'eh BeDarchei HaChayim*, and *Kvurat Chamor*, and Yoel Linetski's Yiddish *Dos Poylishe Yingl*. Professor Graetz's *History of the Jews* also began to appear in Hebrew, and, I believe in Yiddish as well.[3] It appeared in weekly installments, which were avidly (and secretly) gulped down by our young people.

The Dreyfus trial and the Kishinev pogrom had a strong effect on the newly aware youth of the study house. They were beginning to be moved by a national consciousness, and a secret group was organized

[Page 52]

in order to spread new ways of thinking in the Jewish community at large. I, Leyzer Lofer, Shloyme Sharf, Leybl Gosker, and Leyzer Grinberg were among the first organizers of this group. We studied Maimonides and his philosophical works, including his "Guide to the Perplexed," as well as Solomon Rubin, the modern Austrian commentator on the Talmud.[4]

That was when the Bund began sending us its representatives in order to organize a labor union for tailors' apprentices as well as seamstresses. They were the only labor unions in the town.

We also began to convince the young men from the study house to go to Warsaw and make a future for themselves, by learning a trade or becoming shop clerks. These attempts had results. Sometimes the young folks would be "spirited away" in the evenings from their parents.

The first enlightened Jews in Krasnystaw

Standing (r. to l.): Sholem Zinger, Moyshe Shtitser, Dovid Boymfeld, Fayvl Boymfeld (Los Angeles), Leybl Lerman (Chicago), Fishl Helshteyn (Philadelphia), Yoysef Mayman (Winnipeg), Alter Hofman (New York). Seated: Berl Mayman (Winnipeg), Tsisvia Lope, Ben Tsukerman (Los Angeles), Itta Levkovitsh (Canada), Mordkhe Levkovitsh.

[Page 53]

The parents quickly figured out where their children were.

There were some tragic scenes, and those responsible soon found themselves in trouble. Many people felt that taking a young man away from the Talmud and sending him to Warsaw was a terrible thing to do, even though the home was poor and one less person would have helped the others. When I tried to reassure the father of one of my friends by saying that his missing son was well taken care of, and would become a hat-maker, he said, "It would be far better for him to starve while studying Talmud than for him to desecrate Shabbat in Warsaw."

The religious zealots of the town started an open war against the heretics, as they termed us. People were denounced for disseminating Bundist literature. One such denunciation even led to our brief arrest. This war, which was vitriolic, added excitement to our town. One Shabbat, the Hasidim delayed the Torah reading until we "sinners" could be excommunicated and thrown out of the study house.

Over time, we gained some support from the "ignoramuses," the term the Hasidim used for peddlers and artisans. These groups began to understand what we were doing and were won over to our side in the fight against fanaticism and darkness.

Zionism, which had just begun to appear in the town, did not have a great effect on our young people. This was because the movement was elitist, weak, and did not penetrate the smaller towns of Poland.

The Jewish population of Krasnystaw, which numbered about 250, consisted of members of various Hasidic sects, many artisans, a few wealthy people, very little industry, as well as some government suppliers and lumber merchants. There were also the usual religious functionaries: the ritual slaughterer, rabbi, expert in Jewish law, melameds, synagogue managers, and scribes. Their economic situation was always poor. The slaughterers subsisted by collecting the government tax on kosher slaughtering.[5] The rabbi and legal expert barely made enough money to survive. The yeast-selling concessions yielded very little. However, there were heated arguments about the religious functionaries. Factions in the town supported different candidates for the position of rabbi. The meetings about the collection of money to supply the poor with matza on Pesach (Passover) were also fiery. The "middle class" demanded that the flour for Pesach be heavily taxed to help the matza fund.

[Page 54]

However, such taxation always produced the opposite results. The poor, who had large families, used proportionally more flour and matza than the rich; they couldn't afford such "luxury" items as meat, fish etc. and hence consumed large amounts of matza. Thus, they paid their taxes, and the rich paid less into the fund.

This, more or less, was our life in the town until 1907, when I left Krasnystaw and emigrated to America.

The new winds of change that were sweeping Europe at the time, as well as the influence of various ideologies – the "isms" – affected our young people. They were aroused by movements such as Po'alei-Tsiyon, the Bund, Territorialism, and the like.[6] Over time, the young folks broke completely free of religious Orthodox, and joined movements that were suited to their economic conditions.

Emigration from the town steadily increased, although the older generation viewed it unfavorably, especially emigration to America. Ever-intensifying anti-Semitism also strongly influenced the Jews' efforts to emigrate in order to improve their material conditions.

Translator's footnotes:

1. The Haskalah (literally, "wisdom", "erudition" or "education"), often termed the Jewish Enlightenment, was an intellectual movement among the Jews of Central and Eastern Europe. It arose as an ideological worldview during the 1770s and ended around 1881, with the rise of Jewish emancipation in Europe.
2. *HaTsfira* (from the Aramaic word 'tsafra', meaning "morning") was the first Hebrew newspaper, beginning as a weekly in Warsaw (1862), then relocating to Berlin and finally returning to Warsaw as a daily. It appeared until 1931. *Der Fraynd* ('the friend') was the first Yiddish daily in the Russian Empire (1903-1912). The text erroneously states that Asher Ginzburg was the editor; the editor was Shaul Ginzburg.

Memorial Book of the Martyrs of Krasnystaw

3. These influential works marked the beginning of the Jewish Enlightenment. The first four novels, in Hebrew, and the last novel, in Yiddish, were published during the second half of the 19th century. The historian Heinrich Graetz's monumental work was published between 1853 and 1870 and was soon translated into Hebrew and Yiddish.
4. Solomon Rubin, 1823-1910.
5. A 'ritual slaughterer' or Shochet is an expert in the Jewish religious laws governing preparation of kosher meat. The tax was imposed on kosher meat in Poland during the 18th- 19th century.
6. Territorialism was a Jewish movement in the early 20th century that sought to find an alternative territory to Palestine for the creation of a Jewish state.

[Page 55]

A Few Memories

by L. Grinberg (Winnipeg, Canada)

Krasnystaw was not large, compared with its "sister cities" of Chelm, Hrubieszow, etc. However, it differed from them in the proportion of Jews in the population, which was smaller than in the above-mentioned towns. Yet Krasnystaw was famous for its beauty, cleanliness, and its nice, honest, quiet people. As the saying goes, "Don't look at the jar but at what's in it."[1]

The town consisted of two large squares, one inside the other. I term the inner square "the first." The first square had beautiful stone houses, three or four stories tall, with nice paint outside. There was a very beautiful park in the town center, with pedestrian paths. The park center had a lovely, artistic bower, where the army band would perform in the summer almost every evening between 6 and 10.

City Hall was prominent in the cityscape, crowned by the town clock at the top of its tower. The streets of the first square intersected with the streets of the second square at the corners of City Hall. This was a lovely area, though not as beautiful as the first square. The entire town was paved, with a broad sidewalk that extended from the houses to the middle of the street. The sidewalks were lined with trees, most of which had been planted by the town. Gutters separated the sidewalks from the road. All the paved surfaces were slightly sloped, to facilitate water flow

[Page 56]

into the two rivers that surrounded the town. There was never any mud in the town, even after the heaviest rainstorms; it always looked freshly washed. The town overlooked the rivers, and everything poured into the rivers.

Just outside town, on the way to the Lublin road there were beautiful large and small houses. These included small palaces and private homes, as well as government buildings, such as the court, post office, bank, county offices, government schools, and a high school. The area was also the location of the jail and the army barracks.

All these structures occupied a fine, large area.

The three main roads (to Zamość, Rejowiec, and Lublin) endowed the town with beauty, movement, and liveliness.

The loveliest road, that to Lublin, stretched for several miles outside the town and was flanked by trees. Pretty courtyards and various fruit orchards filled the road with fragrance. Meadows, as well as high, imposing, high mountains circled the rivers, and pine forests were nearby. All these features affected the life and character of the town and its population, especially the Jews. The phrase "Jews live on air," meaning without land, was never as apt as for the Jews of Krasnystaw…

Hassids of all the sects of Poland were common in all the towns of the area, as they comprised most of the Jewish population. This was also the case in Krasnystaw. However, the Hassids of Krasnystaw were unusual: they were less pensive, less preoccupied and less bedraggled. On the contrary: they were neat and well-dressed as they walked in groups through the promenades of the town park, without gesticulating or grimacing. Their conversations were wide-ranging, and covered Hassidism, Talmudic debates, Kabbala, philosophy, Hassidic tales, politics, and local as well as world news. These conversations sometimes extended until dawn; people forgot to eat supper and even neglected to join evening prayers. It was almost morning when some of them gathered near a tree for evening prayers. All this took place quietly, with no fuss, without arguments or squabbles. People were calm, quiet, and respectful towards each other.

This general feeling of peace between the Hassidic groups was aided by the presence of the two study houses that were relatively far from the current beautiful city center. They had replaced the older institutions that had served the earlier Jewish population, but the one closest to the Jewish center had burned down. At this time, the Turisk Hassids, who constituted the majority of the Jewish as well as the Hassidic population, were also

[Page 57]

the wealthiest in town. They built themselves a large stone structure in the center of town to serve as their synagogue. After the conflagration, this synagogue became a study house for all the local Jews. People had to tolerate each other's customs, and respect each other's leaders. People even listened to tales of the other group's miracle worker. Thus, a wide-ranging Hassidic "family" was formed. Young men as well as older study house regulars sat together and studied in company. The charming, inspiring voices of these students could be heard throughout the vicinity of the study house. It became famous in the region thanks to its devoted students, who were well educated in both Hassidic and worldly topics.

All this came to an abrupt end during 1904-1906 when the Enlightenment began to spread. That period deserves at least one dedicated chapter.

Translator's footnote:

1. A quote from Mishna Avot 4:20 ("The Sayings of the Fathers"): "Looks can be deceptive."

[Page 58]

The First Emigrants from Krasnystaw in America

by Ben Tsukerman

In 1908, a group of Krasnystaw natives visited me in my modest apartment in the Bronx, New York. Among them were my friend Max Kohn, who was known in our town as Mordkhe-Peysekh of Kosyan, a village near Krasnystaw.

Max bashfully took a letter out of his bag, a letter from a Krasnystaw native living in the Jewish settlement of Lipton, Saskatchewan, in western Canada.[1] His friend, Mendele Shifer, wrote that Jews in western Canada were farming on the 160 acres of arable soil granted free of charge to each Jewish family by the Canadian government. Certain conditions were attached to this grant: each person who received land had to live there for at least six months out of the year, and farm at least ten acres. People who adjusted to these conditions for three years were granted title to the land, and became citizens.

Reading between the lines of this letter, it was clear that the information was propaganda. The writer wanted to sell his farm and therefore painted a rosy picture of life in Lipton, the new land of milk and honey, in the midst of the Canadian prairie. However, we young and inexperienced Jewish idealists, fresh from Poland, did not notice this.

We discovered many drawbacks to America. Jewish immigrants experienced the sweatshops, peddling, the tumult, and the stresses of striving for money.

[Page 59]

Radicalism, whose adherents were led by Binyomin Faygenboym, as well as the Yom Kippur "balls" of the so-called freethinkers, who actually thought of nothing at all, were depressing for such young Jewish immigrants as us, who came from the small towns of Poland.

Therefore, as we talked in my apartment, we developed a detailed plan for a cooperative settlement. We resolved to flee New York and become physical laborers in Canada. Max Kohn was given the task of writing to Mendele Shifer and asking for more information.

We soon left for Winnipeg, the gateway to western Canada. When we arrived, we were met by an immigration official who had been notified by telegram that we were coming. He greeted us in Yiddish, and led us into a lovely, well-kept, warm immigrant facility that was run by the government. Our group of six was immediately heartened: it was no small thing to be greeted by Mr. Goodman, an official representative with a rosette on his uniform, who spoke a sweet Yiddish. He looked us up and down with his penetrating gaze, and told us that Lipton was about five hundred miles from Winnipeg, and that before leaving we should meet with Mr. Hefner, the ICA representative, who would best advise us how to proceed.[2] He himself was very skeptical of our plans. Looking at us again, he said in a fatherly tone, "Children, stay in Winnipeg. You'll find it much easier to settle in." My wife agreed with Mr. Goodman, and tried to convince us to settle in Winnipeg, among other Jews. But the four of us from Krasnystaw did not want to change our plans. We decided to meet Hefner, the ICA representative; and then would proceed to Lipton regardless of any difficulties he might create.

It was November, 1908. The winds in western Canada were fierce and the cold increased day by day. We visited Mr. Hefner, who greeted us warmly. He was a veteran settler, originally from Russia, who had a large farm in Canada. He considered us, and said, "Children, you're naïve. You'll be miserable, soon grow disillusioned, and abandon the land. It's not suitable for you." He smiled, and turned to me, saying, "Young man, show me your hands." As he looked at my hands, he added, a bit sarcastically,

[Page 60]

"Your hands were meant for turning the pages of the Talmud, not for agricultural work." However, we dug our heels in and would not give up on our plans.

We left Winnipeg two days later, and arrived in Lipton on Nov. 15. The town numbered about 200 residents, forty or fifty of whom were Jews.

We met with a Jewish shopkeeper who had connections to the Jewish settlers. This was Moyshe Baldan, a wise and educated man from Bessarabia. He took pity on us, and advised us to return to New York if we could afford it, or to Winnipeg. The brutal life on the prairies was not suited to Jews, especially for those who had come from New York. He invited us to supper, and during the meal recounted the history of Jewish settlement in western Canada. He was very knowledgeable, as he was one of the first Jewish settlers who had arrived from Bessarabia after the Kishinev pogrom.[3]

In 1903, the JCA, together with the government of Canada, funded 200 Jewish families from Romania and settled them in the area of Lipton, Cooper, and Deysert, Saskatchewan.[4] The newcomers were not suited to farming; they were mostly Jews who had specific occupations. "Aunt JCA" wanted to turn them into peasants, but had forgotten to supply them with specifically Jewish institutions such as a shochet, a mohel, a melamed, a mikvah, etc.[5] The Christian manager, McNab, was not familiar with the needs of a Jewish community, nor was he interested in them. Once, when he received an order for Passover matzah, the matzah arrived on the second day of Shavuot...[6] The Jewish farmers from Romania, who respected the anniversaries of their deceased relatives, requested a delivery of memorial candles. McNab brought in a wagon full of candles.

Moyshe Baldan reported many such tragicomic incidents, in order to discourage us from going to the village. We spent the night at his home. The next morning, we saw several Jewish settlers who came to buy some goods at his shop. They looked at us with a mixture of disdain and pity. "Well, guys," one of them called to us, "if you want to become miserable, come with me. I'll take you to Mendele Shifer." It was midnight before we arrived at Mendele Shifer's place, whose letters had inspired us to become settlers. We woke him up. His house was filthy, as he lived alone; his wife and children were still in Poland. We were extremely hungry and tired after our journey. He offered

[Page 61]

my wife his bed for a rest, and we men sat down at the table to talk. But my wife was unable to touch the squalid bed and sat at the long table with us to discuss practicalities.

Mendele asked us to talk quietly, because the children – his students – were asleep under the table. It became clear that, besides a farmer, he was also the melamed, and the letter-writer for the Jewish farmers, men and women, who could not write in the local language.

Our spokesman Max Kohn, asked him, "How is it possible? Where is your decency? How could a man like you exaggerate so much? How could you have written that the land was free, supplied with geese, hens, ducks, cows, and horses – and the upshot is a big nothing?"

"Yes," Mendele Shifer answered calmly. "All these good things are available. There is enough land, but it is a thousand miles away. There are geese, ducks, hens, cows and horses here, but they're owned by the German settlers who arrived ten or fifteen years ago… On the other hand, we JCA-supported folks are having a hard time. I did not tell any lies…I believed that at least one of you would have several thousand dollars, and I would sell my farm and go home to my family in Poland, in Tomaszow-Lubelski. But don't despair: you will all find jobs with the Jewish settlers here…"

During this conversation, we noticed a sausage hanging in one of the corners. We stared at it hungrily. I had stayed silent until then, but now my hunger compelled me to speak. "Reb Mendele," I turned to him, "How about some food?" I pointed at the sausage. Reb Mendele stroked his black beard with its silver strand and responded in a chant like that of Talmudic scholars: "Children, the sausage is for Shabbat. Go to the garden and dig up the radishes that I planted last spring."

Needless to say, no one slept that night. We all felt duped, but no one said a word. We had no choice but to hire ourselves out to a few of the Jewish settlers as laborers. My wife and I hired ourselves out to a Romanian Jewish farmer named Zelik Yoyneh for three months, in return for one hundred dollars.

The Romanian Jews had been living on their farms for many years but had not amounted to anything. Their young folks had left for the big cities to work or study, and the members of the older generation gradually left their farms. Only a few had stayed on the land, prospered, and become rich.

The Baron's support of Jewish farmers seemed to be cursed. All the JCA officials

[Page 62]

were assimilated Parisian Jews, who treated our Jews with condescension and hostility. They had not made sure to meet the spiritual needs of the settlers and treated them like stepchildren. Therefore, the colonists did not trust them and cheated wherever possible.

One of the settlers had a photograph of a group of settlers with the Canadian Minister of Agriculture, standing in a freshly plowed field. The settler was proud of the picture and told me that he had waited to plow those four acres until the photograph was taken.

The Jews had more spiritual needs than other peasants, needs that are vital. If the JCA administrators had understood, the results would have been much better. However, they did not, or could not, understand. The land was unyielding, and the officials of the JCA – no less so.

We Jews were still the People of the Book. Economic development must go hand in hand with spiritual development; that is a prerequisite for successful settlement. The best example of this is in the Land of Israel.

It is therefore not surprising that most of the settlers eventually left their farms. We immigrants from Krasnystaw were among them. Regardless of our steadfast idealism, we had to return to our towns, which promised a better spiritual existence.

[Page 63]

[Blank]

Translator's footnotes:

1. Jews lived in this village but were not a majority.
2. The Jewish Colonization Association (JCA or ICA)), was an organization created in 1891 by Baron Maurice de Hirsch. Its aim was to facilitate the mass emigration of Jews from Russia and other Eastern European countries, by settling them in agricultural settlements on lands

purchased by the committee in North America (Canada and the United States), South America (Argentina and Brazil) and Ottoman Palestine.
3. The pogrom that started on Easter Sunday, April 19, 1903 in modern-day Chișinău (Yiddish Kishinev), Moldova, is considered a major event in modern Jewish history. 49 Jews were killed, 92 were gravely injured, a number of Jewish women were raped, over 500 were lightly injured, and 1,500 homes were damaged.
4. The writer mentions two other settlements in Saskatchewan, which I have not been able to identify, and have transliterated their names from the Yiddish.
5. A shochet or 'ritual slaughterer' is an expert on Jewish laws governing what is kosher and prepares kosher meat. A mohel performs the Jewish rite of circumcision. The melamed is a teacher of Jewish subjects for school children. A mikvah is a 'ritual bath' used to fulfill Jewish obligations for ritual purity.
6. The holiday of Shavuot (Yiddish: Shevues) is seven weeks after Passover.

[Page 64]

Personalities

[Page 65]

A Name Enveloped in Sanctity

by A. Gelberg

"The Zygelboym Book" compiled by Y. S. Hertz. Title page art by Y. Shloss. 408 pages, pictures. Published with the aid of the Bund members in Mexico, by "Undzer Tsayt," New York, 1947.[1]

The conventional amount of reviews and critiques is impossible for a book of this kind, especially one devoted to Zygelboym. In its 408 pages of text, and additional pictures, we must make sure that the compiler included all the material relating to the significant stages of our hero's life, arranged and sorted so as to present us with the most important features of the person who will be known eternally as the martyr Arthur Zygelboym.

The compiler, Y. S. Hertz, seems to have done so in most of the book. His introductory words, presented below, lead us to an elevated, clear place of sanctity and admiration.

"He rose from the depths of the people to the highest peaks of the nation's dreams. He was one of the vanguard who leaped to war first, ready for sacrifice. The pages of this book contain his thoughts and feelings. Let us once again hear his heartbeat, let his voice sound again

[Page 66]

and his figure not dissappear from our vision. Life breathes once again through his words and deeds."

Reading the first 29 pages, in which Hertz describes the course of his life, the link to his suicide in London is logical. The last words of his farewell letter, "I cannot be silent. I cannot live while the remnants of the Jewish population of Poland, of whom I am a representative, are perishing," are a fitting final expression for this son of the nation, whose life was dedicated to the joys and sorrows of his people. When his people were murdered, his own physical existence was impossible; when death and murder reigned, continuing his own life was immoral.

This is clear from his articles, which are assembled in this memorial book under the heading "The Man and the Movement." The essays radiate the socialist ethic dreamed of by generations and longed for by all those for whom the concept of Socialism is different from the game played by the authorities and the seekers of state or imperial power. The essays delineate Arthur as Bundist, and his socialist heart.

The book also includes Zygelboym's essay for the Yiddish General Encyclopedia, which deals with the Jewish professional movement in Poland. This important essay is written very correctly.[2]

The most dramatic part of the book is that which describes the first part of the vicious German rule over Warsaw, and the writer's escape abroad through Nazi Germany, of all routes. One reads the 211 pages that delineate the early German occupation with bated breath. In contrast, the account of his flight through Germany is written in a matter-of-fact tone. The descriptions, which are often quite colorful, constitute another book about the beginning of our devastation, and help us to understand the later development of the catastrophe. Most importantly, they tell us about the of the heroes who later gave their lives in the service of heroic resistance and death.

The 69 pages that constitute the most tragic section of the book contain materials and documents under the heading "For the Ears of the World." They present Arthur's appearance in international forums, his activity as the Bund representative in Poland's government-in-exile in London, and his desperate appeals to the deaf, indifferent world to stop the Nazi crimes

[Page 67]

against the Jews of Poland. These documents sear, for all eternity, the brand of shame onto mankind (in addition to Germany, the cannibal), shame for a period that was one of utter lack of scruples and unbelievable human depravity.

The Arthur Zygelbojm memorial book concludes with a section of poetry and epic poems by Z. Shneour, Arn Glatnz-Leyeles, Zusman Segalovitch, Avrom Nochem Shtentsl, and Władysław Broniewski, as well as a series of pictures. It is a tragic, sacred book.[3]

Yiddish journalism has often argued about whether Zygelboym's behavior was proper, especially in light of his socialist and Bundist beliefs. His suicide impelled some scholars to see his suicide as the philosophical end to one ideology of Jewish life, rather than excitement and enthusiasm about the future of our history. The book also includes letters, proclamations, and eulogies of people such as Jan Karski, Professor Kot, H. Leyvik, Zygmunt Nowakowski, Marek Orczynski, and others (in addition to Arthur's family).[4] It is these connections that add an aura of sanctity to Zygelboym's name.

As we learn from Orczynski's article, "the recent tragic death of the ardent Bund idealist, Deputy Zygelboym, has shaken the English-speaking world... This action has become a turning point in the attitude of the Allies to this issue. Since then, Poland received various types of aid, which helped the rescue operations. Understanding the severity of the problem was followed by requests for information about the condition of Jews in Poland."

We know that the assistance was great, and we, of course, witnessed the end... Characteristically, Arthur's last bang of his head against the solid wall sounded loudly in the deaf ears. However, the main thing that we and the coming generations will realize is that his suicide was not only a last act of desperation, a last theatrical gesture to jolt the conscience of the world, but, more importantly, an act of profound devotion and love towards his people. It was a love that overcame the boundary between life and death.

This was the figure of Arthur Zygelboym. Thus was his character formed. The Zygelboym book is a well-balanced work that is worthy of his multifaceted personality.

Translator's footnotes:

1. Shmuel Mordkhe ("Arthur") Zygelbojm (Zygelboym, 1895-1943) was a Polish socialist politician, Bund activist, and member of the National Council of the Polish government-in-exile. He committed suicide after the Warsaw Ghetto was crushed as a protest against the inaction of the Western allies. He and his family moved to Krasnystaw in 1899. "Arthur" was his code name. In this text, I have presented his last name in English transliteration.

2. *Di Algemeyne Entsiklopedye* (*The General Encyclopedia*) was a Yiddish language publishing project created in Berlin, Paris and New York between 1932 and 1966.

3. Zalman Shneour (1887–1959) was one of the most prolific and popular Yiddish and Hebrew writers between the world wars. The Yiddish writer Arn Glantz-Leyeles (1889-1966) wrote prose as A. Glantz and poetry as A. Leyeles. Zusman Segalovitch (1884–1949) was a Yiddish poet, novelist, and journalist. Avrom Nochem Shtentsl (1897-1984) wrote Yiddish prose and poetry. Władysław Broniewski (1897-1962) was a Polish poet, writer, and translator known for his patriotic writings. For more see the YIVO Archives website entry "Guide to the Papers of Shmuel Mordkhe (Artur) Zygielbojm".

4. Jan Karski (1914-2000) was an underground courier for the Polish government-in-exile who delivered evidence of the mass murder of European Jews to the western Allies and reported on Nazi atrocities in the Warsaw ghetto and on the deportation of Jews to killing centers. Stanysław Kot (1881-1975) was a Polish historian and politician. H. Leivik (1888-1962) was a prolific Yiddish writer, best known for *The Golem*, his 1921 "dramatic poem in eight scenes." Zygmunt Nowakowski (1891-1963) was a Polish famous actor, theatrical director, and philologist. I could not identify Marek Orczynski.

Memorial Book of the Martyrs of Krasnystaw

[Page 68]

Shmuel Mordkhe Zygielbojm (Arthur): A Biography[1]

by Y. Sh. Hertz

Shmuel Mordkhe Zygielbojm was born on September 21, 1895, in the village of Borowice, Lublin province, near Krasnistaw. He spent his first four years in that village.

The family moved to the nearby town of Krasnystaw in 1899, where Shmuel Mordkhe lived until he was fourteen. His childhood years were difficult.

[Page 69]

His father, Yoysef, known in the town as Yoske Teacher, was a dedicated smoker. He was sickly, tall and thin, and coughed constantly. The man, with his distinctive yellowish, pointed little beard was well known to the young people and the general population. He taught them how to read and write. Though Yoske Teacher was religiously observant, he was considered modern, as he read secular books and newspapers.

Shmuel Mordkhe's tall, broad-shouldered mother, Henya, was the daughter of Yekl the ritual slaughterer, who was also the mohel and cantor in the town's study house. The frail Yoske Teacher could not feed the family, and their survival fell to Henya. She came from a family of scholars; she herself was a seamstress who made dresses on her Singer sewing machine. She was therefore known in the town as Henya the Seamstress. The mother's strong hands and shoulders were the pillars of the home, into which boys and girls were born, eleven in all.

Yet both occupations, teaching and sewing, combined, were not enough to feed the family. Shmuel Mordkhe's childhood was one of hunger and shortage. Yet he enjoyed as much childish joy as was then possible in this town. They lived near the Wieprz River, near the synagogue of the Turisk Hassids. The beauty and fascination of the river joined the prayers and song of the Hassids to create an atmosphere of fantasy for the child.

It might have been here, on the banks of the Wieprz, that Shmuel Mordkhe began to develop his thoughts and feelings for the people of Poland. Their landlord was Christian. The father and mother barely earned enough to feed their large family, let alone pay rent. However, the Christian landlord was kind enough to let them live in the apartment rent-free. This was probably a major factor of young Zygielbojm's positive attitude to Gentiles.

Shmuel Mordkhe studied in the kheyder until the age of ten, after which he continued on to Talmud study. However, he did not become a scholar.

His interests lay elsewhere, though he was considered a gifted student. He learned quickly, yet he was not interested in his subjects. His heart and mind called him to the street, the river, the fields, pranks, games, and dreams.

He was always the leader of his classmates, from early childhood on. He

[Page 70]

was very energetic and was the leader in every project.

His family was so poor that he, the grandson of Yekl the religious leader, could not continue his studies. At that time, several Krasnystaw Jews formed a partnership and opened a large factory that manufactured wooden pill containers. Some people in town said that the boxes were designed to hold ointments for filthy people suffering from skin diseases. The factory was in the Grablie quarter, the poorest in town, across the Wieprz and near the road to Zamość. It employed some one hundred workers, almost all of them children. The children came mostly from poor families of Grablie, except for some from across the river, whose families had been well off but had become impoverished. One of the latter was Yoske Teacher's little boy, whose family couldn't afford to pay tuition, and who wasn't interested in further education in the study house.

Both boys and girls worked at the factory. The boys cut the thin strips of wood for the boxes, and the girls glued them together to make round containers. They earned twenty or thirty groschen a day.[2] Shmuel Mordkhe would bring all of his earnings home, as his contribution to the family. He was always hungry. This was the impetus for one of his exploits at the factory, which made him many friends among the children but annoyed the owners.

One day, the workers realized that the glue used to make the boxes had become useless. The glued strip ends separated. An investigation revealed the reason: the flour was always mixed with some soft cheese. One day, 11 year-old Shmuel Mordkhe showed his hungry co-workers that they could add less cheese to the flour, and could enjoy the leftover cheese. The children began doing so. The children gradually reduced the amount of cheese in the glue, until the disaster occurred. When the owners discovered what was happening, one of them, Chayim Borekh the wood merchant, found a primitive solution. He spat into the mixture of cheese and flour while the children looked on; they then gave up the habit.

Young Zygielbojm had a terrible experience one day, when the angel of death hovered nearby. He was very capable and volunteered to do things that went beyond his abilities. He was given one of the most responsible – and most dangerous – tasks in the factory: operating a wood slicer that ensured the proper size of the strips. He accidentally

[Page 71]

sliced off the tips of two fingers, cutting through flesh and bone. That was the first time he was exposed to such danger. His fingers healed, but his flat fingertips were a constant reminder of the accident and pain he had experienced. Shortly after this mishap, the boy started working for pay in his aunt's bakery. He worked there for some time and left; he was only twelve.

That was the end of his childhood at home. From now on, constant poverty dictated his actions. In 1907, the boy went into the world, first to the big city of Warsaw, without the care and love of parents, all alone into a roiling sea of people at a very fraught time. But he realized that he could no longer rely on the meager shoulders of his ailing father, while his hardworking mother produced more children who required her constant attention and drained her of energy. He hoped to become independent and support himself, and try his luck in the enormous hubbub of Warsaw. Shmuel Mordkhe Zygielbojm spent seven years of his youth in the metropolis, years that were lean, and hadn't been preceded by years of plenty.[3]

He learned a new trade in Warsaw, apprenticing himself to a glove-maker. He lived with his master for a while, doing all the household chores, and often being beaten. This made him so desperate that he once fled from the house and lived on the street for a week, spending nights on a bench in the Krasiński Garden. He later found lodging with a family from Krasnystaw that had moved to Warsaw, on Karmelicka Street (later called Lubeckiego Street), in a poor part of town. The impoverished woman from Krasnystaw (a sister of Menachem Rozenboym, who later became known as a Bundist activist) knew Shmuel Mordkhe from their hometown, and provided help and support in his time of need.

The adolescent young man liked to write poetry in his free time. His "poetic creations" did not only meet his need to express his thoughts and moods and foster his hope to become well known but were also a way to pass the time. The young glove-maker was unemployed for months. The best day of the week was Shabbat, when natives of Krasnystaw living in Warsaw would gather for companionship, and to hear the latest news from home. They were Shmuel Mordkhe's audience, listened to his poetry, gave their critiques, and sometimes encouraged him. And, though his friends

[Page 72]

advised him to take the poems to a publisher, he did not have the courage to do that.

His life changed radically with the outbreak of World War I, when he decided to return to Krasnystaw. But he did not stay there long; his family left the town in 1915 due to the effects of the battles between the Russian and Austrian forces and settled in Chelm. That is where he began his social activism, to which he devoted himself with all his heart, and for which he eventually gave up his life.

At the mature age of 20, Shmuel Mordkhe began to serve in a Russian military hospital. He now became acquainted with two very smart physicians, who encouraged him to acquire an education. Very soon, he became passionately interested in the developing Jewish labor movement.

As a child in the pillbox factory in Krasnystaw, he had experienced a strike. During his Warsaw years, 1907-1914, he took part in economic actions. He also participated in a political protest strike announced by the Bund, in connection with the blood-libel trial initiated in Kiev by the Czarist government.[4] He was not, however, a member of the Bund. The first Bundists he encountered were the leaders of the glovemakers' union in Warsaw, but he never became close to the organization. His general inclination was nationalist; he did not believe in Socialism at all. His feelings were profoundly changed in 1915, in Chelm.

When Austrian forces took over Chelm, the labor movement emerged from its clandestine existence and its numbers increased. Veteran Bundists in Chelm from the period of Russian rule, who had survived all of the Czarist repressions as well as persecutions by Jewish informants and collaborators, were murdered in 1906-1907, in the local manner.[5] Informers supplied a list of those who read the Bund's newspapers; everyone on the list was arrested.

Once the town was under Austrian control, a "workers' home" was established for members of various parties.[6] Zygielboym was elected a member of the organization's leadership. It was the first arena of his social activities. The "workers' home" later came under Bund control and attracted most of the city's Jewish workers. At that time, the Bundist

[Page 73]

activists Dr. Mirlas of Warsaw and Dr. S. Fensterbloy of Cracow, who had served in the local garrison as an Austrian army officer during the occupation, were living there at the time. Zygielbojm threw himself enthusiastically into the practical aspects of the Jewish labor movement, which was flourishing.

The first convention of Bundist organizations in Poland was held in Lublin at the end of December 1917. At the time, Poland was occupied by Germany and Austro-Hungary. The Bundists of Chelm sent Zygielbojm as their delegate. This was the young activist's first chance to meet the most important leaders and members of the Bund. He made a very good impression with his factual report on his city, and his deep interests in the issues being discussed. He was particularly interested in the question of nationalities and asked the convention for clarification. This interest stemmed from his personal strong Jewish national feeling, as well as from the situation in Chelm, where there were residents of three nationalities: Jews, Poles, and Ukrainians. At that moment, there was a strong conflict between Poland and Ukraine over Chelm.

The Chelm Bundist movement grew, and Zygielbojm was one of its most capable and active members. The Bundist organization was able to obtain a building for itself and for the professional unions aligned with it. This achievement was largely thanks to Zygielbojm's efforts. The movement's ongoing growth spurred him to more social activism.

His private life, however, was marked by poverty. He had married during the war and continued to work as a glovemaker. His wife Golda was a seamstress. Their earnings were so meager that they could afford only a basement apartment. He divided his time between the large building of the movement and the basement, where he, Golda, and their first child, Yosef-Leyb, lived.

His hard life as well as the constant party activity that occupied him day and night did not stop the young activist from continuing his own education. Although his father was a teacher, Zygielbojm had not received a regular education, and lacked even basic knowledge. He now began to devote energy to catching up with what he had missed in his childhood and youth. In Chelm, he became friendly with a young Polish female intellectual (the wife of the veteran Socialist, Professor Zygmunt Hering), who began to teach him Polish. He later continued his studies and mastered the language.

Zygielbojm left Chelm in 1920 and settled in Warsaw. This marked the start

[Page 74]

of wide-ranging new activities. The large number of Jewish workers allowed him to increase his capacities and develop his authorial, speaking, and organizational skills. The name of Zygielbojm did not become well known among Jewish workers in Warsaw, but his party alias, Comrade Artur, quickly gained popularity.

It was the period of the Polish-Russian war. The Bundist movement was being harshly repressed, and new activists were vital. The central committee decided to admit the young provincial activist to its ranks. He was soon given two responsible positions: secretary of the Jewish metal workers' professional union, and a member of the Warsaw Bund committee. This marked the beginning of his rapid rise within the movement. Zygielbojm soon became one of the central activists of the Jewish Labor movement in Poland.

He would leave his apartment every morning and enter the crush of the poor Jews who lived on Stawki Street, returning late at night, after a day of exciting experiences, many impressions and efforts, making new acquaintances and encountering new problems.

Artur tried his hand in several fields. He was active in politics as well as in propaganda and rose to the highest levels in both areas. He proved to be an organizer, teacher, and writer -- talents not often found in the same person.

During the first decade of his Bundist activities in Warsaw, he took up major positions in the movement. At the party convention of December 1924, he was elected a member of the Bund's Central Committee and continued to be a major figure of the movement's leadership; he was re-elected at each convention.

The office of Secretary of the Jewish metalworkers' union was the beginning of his professional activity. He later attained higher positions. For a time, he was the Secretary of the Council of Jewish Professional Unions in Warsaw and thus was in touch with Jewish workers in various professions, learning about their lives and needs, and familiarizing himself with their efforts and struggles. In this capacity, he was able to connect Jewish and Polish workers in the Warsaw council of professional unions.

Zygielbojm was also active in the national council of professional unions of Jewish workers (the association of Polish Jewish workers).

[Page 75]

As a member and long-time Secretary of the National Council, he was able to influence the work of all the professional unions of Jewish workers in Poland. Until 1930, he was also the editor of *Workers' Problems*, the journal of the Jewish workers.

This was not all his professional activity. He carried out two more important functions. For over ten years, beginning in 1926, he was the chairman of the national professional union of leather workers. This organization included Jewish, Polish, and other non-Jewish workers. He made a remarkable contribution to the development and growth of the International Professional Union, which significantly helped shoemakers, tanners, and other leather workers in Poland to improve their conditions.

As a member of the leather workers' union, Zygielbojm spent many years as a member of the highest authority of the nation-wide professional union: the Central Committee of the Federation of all professional unions in Poland, which included all professional workers, regardless of national affiliation. Beginning in 1924, he was a member of the Central Committee of Professional Unions. His contributions, in word and deed, helped to develop the Polish Labor movement.

Beginning in 1927, a new field of social activity became available. That year, there were elections to a new Warsaw city council. The Warsaw Bund slated him as a candidate. Together with other Bund leaders, he was elected by the Jewish workers of Warsaw as their representative in the city administration. As a member of the Warsaw City Council, he justified the trust placed in him and carried out the position admirably. The role of city council member was extremely important, because the Warsaw city council dealt not only with community matters but was also a top political expression of the mood in the country's capital.

Many Bund activists traveled to the cities and towns of Poland. Strikes, election campaigns, party conventions, and other important occasions, as well as general lectures, were reasons for such visits by important activists. Zygielbojm was one of these frequent travelers. In addition to carrying out his mission, he always brought news. He was not only interested in the local affairs that had direct bearing on his mission; his experienced, perceptive gaze penetrated the depths of local life and sensed local features. After returning to Warsaw, he wrote down his impressions of everyday life in provincial areas, and

[Page 76]

published them in the Bundist press as Z. Artur. The writer in him could not remain passive in the face of these portraits of daily life, or stay silent about the mistreatment by petty strongmen and local fixers, whom he called "Berl Kutshmes". In speech as well as in writing, Artur was not only persuasive but also inspiring and uplifting.

The Jewish Labor movement in Poland was multifaceted, tumultuous and emotional. It provided people with an outlet for their talents. Organizers and speakers, theoreticians and writers were able to express themselves. Not everyone could pass the test of public perception of the

Labor movement; and not all those who passed the test had the will to continue the highly demanding work that was required. Many lacked the stamina, and perhaps the idealism as well, needed to survive the difficult struggle of the Jewish Labor movement.

During the grim period of need and loneliness that Zygielbojm suffered during his childhood and youth, he constantly dreamed of distinguishing himself. He set himself serious goals and strove to achieve them. He was very grateful to the Bund for providing him with the chance to set free his latent powers, develop his capabilities, and be of service. Although the young man achieved much very quickly and became one of the main leaders of the movement, and believed in his powers and abilities, he was never smug about his achievements. On the contrary, he always felt some unhappiness. This was not a result of any bitterness but rather stemmed from low self-esteem. The Jewish Labor movement was distinguished by its broad scope and strong idealism but was far from perfect. The sober realist in him went hand in hand with the dreamer. He was excellent at judging what could and could not be achieved. Yet he was never satisfied with merely achieving the possible. Constantly striving for greater achievements was in his nature.

He was immersed day and night in his community work, yet he always sought something new. His interest in literature and theater – and cultural activity in general – during the early 1930s led him to spend a year in the United States in order to distribute Jewish books. He continued this work later in Poland, when he became the official representative of the Jewish Encyclopedia.[7]

[Page 77]

He approached the older, veteran leaders of the Bund, whose concept of leadership was extremely democratic and straightforward, with love and respect. The relationship of these leaders to others erased all boundaries between themselves and ordinary party members, and all trace of patronization. Members who looked up to the veteran leaders did so out of pure, profound esteem, great love, and deference.

This was also the case with Artur, who was now part of the movement's leadership. He inspired people to treat the old-time leaders with veneration; they remained his teachers and guides, though his views did not change.

In the Fall of 1936, Artur took his activism elsewhere. He left Warsaw and moved to Lodz.

For years, the acknowledged leader of the working Jews in Poland's largest center of workers had been Yisroel Likhtenshteyn, one of the finest and noblest persons ever to emerge from among the Jews of Poland. The Jewish Labor movement of Lodz, to which Yisroel Likhtenshteyn had devoted his pure heart and sensitive soul, expanded even more after his death in 1933.

The Jewish workers of Lodz produced many outstanding leaders. The local Bund movement – the political party as well as the youth organization – included a large number of youth activists, who expressed their moral strength and capacity during the years of World War II, under the hellish conditions of the ghetto that was established by the Nazi authorities.

Likhtenshteyn, however, was irreplaceable. The large movement required leaders. This led to the idea of relocating a central Bund activist in Lodz. The Bund Central Committee believed that Artur would be the best person for this mission. He was enthusiastic, and, as a loyal member of the organization, carried out the directive of the Central Committee.

He settled in Lodz and began working with all his energy and devotion. Although his official title was Secretary of the Lodz Bund, Artur was connected with all the sections of the Bund. In late 1938, he was elected a member of the Lodz city council; as such, he was authorized to speak in public. His speeches in the city council were remarkably knowledgeable and displayed the movement's principles as well as the militancy that characterized broad swaths of the Jewish workers throughout Poland.

Lodz, the second largest city in Poland, was then headed by a council and

[Page 78]

a judiciary, both with a Socialist majority. The Bund had considerable representation. The minority, however, consisted of staunch, anti-Semitic "Endeks."[8] Zygielbojm's courageous speeches in the Council revealed the reactionary face of the Endeks and their partners, as well as their hatred for the common people. He defended the Jewish population and demonstrated the hypocrisy of the anti-Semitic demagoguery, pitting it against the solidarity of Jewish and Polish workers.

Zygielbojm carried out his important task in Lodz until the storm of war began, in September 1939.

Five days after the start of the war, German forces stood at the gates of Lodz. Faced with this pressure, the Polish forces retreated, along with large portions of the civilian population; all of them headed towards Warsaw. Zygielbojm was part of these crowds.

He was witness to unprecedented, enormous, and terrible events that were happening in and around burning villages, under fire and bombs from the enemy airplanes. These were the terrible conditions of his trip to Warsaw, the city where he spent the best years of his life and developed his social conscience. He came now as a mature man, with almost twenty-five years of turbulent social activity in the Labor Movement which had raised him. Dust and sweat now covered the face that had been furrowed by a hard life.

Impelled by the need to reach Warsaw before the arrival of the swiftly advancing German forces, his thoughts ranged from memories of the near and far past to the terrible images of the panic that had seized the roads and towns between Lodz and Warsaw. At times, he was sometimes able to escape, and distance himself from the nightmarish reality, but the great historical task that destiny had assigned to him was as yet unrevealed. He approached the future with the same questions that occupied him every day.

His arrival in Warsaw radically changed the picture. He saw new tasks that were huge and difficult and happily took them upon himself.

At 2:00 a.m. on Thursday, September 7, 1939, Artur, limping on his swollen feet, neared Warsaw. He came through the

[Page 79]

quarter of Wola, and knocked at the door of his comrade, Avrom Kastelanski, on Leszno Street, where he was able to rest after his arduous journey.

Artur planned to continue eastward, like the tens of thousands of people who believed that somewhere on the other side of the Vistula there would be a strong line of defense to resist Hitler's armored corps. He didn't want to be forced into passivity while the people in the country were actively battling the Nazi terror. He realized that he needed to be better informed about the situation before going any further. With this in mind, he went to the leader of the Polish Socialist Party, Mieczysław Niedziałkowski, and learned that the decision had been reached to surrender Warsaw, the capital, without a fight. The defensive forces were weak, and the prospects of victory meager. Nevertheless, Warsaw would not surrender.

Artur was upset when he returned from his meeting with Niedziałkowski and announced to a few of his close friends that he would not be leaving Warsaw. Tears ran down his face, as he told them that he would stay to help in the defense of the city.

He began working with fresh energy. A group of Party leaders had made a work plan for the next few days. Among other tasks, the Bund's daily newspaper *Folks-Tsaytung* would continue to appear during the siege, which was expected to begin any day. Artur was designated as liaison with the Polish Labor movement, and met daily with Niedziałkowski and Zygmunt Zaremba.[9]

There was much to do. Over one million people lived in Warsaw, among them several hundreds of thousands of Jews. These Jews needed to be disciplined in their fight against the Nazi enemy; they also needed major help in the struggle. Just as among the Poles, the Jewish activists in the three-week-long defensive battle were the workers.

Artur headed this major undertaking. He wrote a call to the Jews to participate in the defense of the city, and to enlist in the volunteer battalions. He wrote a daily article in the *Folks-Tsaytung* about urgent everyday needs, and actively participated in practical aid to the Jewish population.[10]

His work was wide-ranging, from battling the Nazis in the trenches to establishing kitchens for the hungry. Artur was at the head of

[Page 80]

all these efforts. He was also entrusted with representation of the Jews of Warsaw in the city's general defense committee. The best of the young Jewish Socialists, who were members of the young Bundist's Tsukunft organization, were members not only of the armed resistance units, but also of the special fire brigades. Dressed in their organization uniforms, the young Bundists were stationed in attics or on roofs during bombardments, prepared to extinguish fires started by bombs.

The inevitable end came after a heroic, hopeless battle, which the defenders fought to their last breath. After 21 days of battle, Warsaw had no choice but to surrender. At the last moment, Niedziałkowski – the Bund's representative in the defense committee – refused to sign the capitulation document, declaring, "The working class does not surrender." However, this prideful gesture could not change the situation. Warsaw and its brave population were now at the mercy of the Nazi forces. The Jews of Warsaw faced the worst chapter ever to occur in history.

As soon as the enemy entered the city, they demanded twelve representatives of the population as hostages who guarantee with their lives to ensure that the community's obligations would be carried out and that order would be maintained.

The city's president, Stefan Starzyński, who had behaved so admirably during the siege, summoned Ester Iwanska, the Bund activist (Wiktor Alter's sister), and announced that the Jews, too, needed to provide representatives as hostages. He suggested two Bundists and one unaffiliated resident. The outcome of this conversation was that the Jews should supply two representatives, one Bundist and one resident. City president Starzyński demanded that Ester Iwanska be the Bundist hostage.

Her response was that she could not make that decision herself, but had to consult with leading members of the Bund. She promised to return soon with an answer.

A meeting of the leading members was immediately convened. Artur declared that he would never allow a woman to be taken hostage, and actually offered himself as a hostage. The other participants in the meeting agreed. The meeting of Bund leaders had previously discussed whether the Bund should agree in principle to a member's becoming a hostage. They resolved that a member could become a hostage, so as not to abdicate their responsibilities as representatives of the Jewish population.

Comrade Ester went to the city's president, and told him of the

[Page 81]

Bund's decision. President Starzyński did not oppose the change of hostage but pointed out the difficulty of Zygielbojm's status as a non-resident of Warsaw but rather a citizen of Lodz. They finally decided to falsify his documents. He was described as a member of the city council on behalf of the Jewish workers. While Zygielbojm was becoming a hostage in Warsaw, the Gestapo was searching for him in Lodz, where they had already arrested a number of Bund activists.

Thus did Artur volunteer to respond to the first danger, providing himself as a guarantee for the Jews of Warsaw. The second Jewish hostage was Avrom Gefner, the leader of the merchants.

One day in October 1939, the police spread out through Warsaw in search of Zygielbojm. They had several addresses for him, but, as they did not find him anywhere, took temporary hostages instead. Other people were arrested at their homes. Among them was Zygielbojm's first wife, Golda, from whom he had been separated for years.[a] That was when Hitler came to visit the large cities of Poland, and observed his soldiers' victory parade.

As a hostage guaranteeing the good behavior of the population, Zygielbojm was one of the first people to lay the foundation for the underground Jewish Labor movement. The first convention of the underground Bund in Warsaw, the secret organization that was destined to play such a heroic, tragic role, took place in mid-October 1939, about two weeks after the enemy had taken the city. The convention took place in the workers' kitchen on Zamenhof Street, with the participation of twenty-some delegates who represented all the trades. Their first task was to organize connections with all sections of Jewish workers. The delegates sat at the table with bowls of soup, so that a Gestapo raid would think that it was a meal for the poor. Artur opened the founding convention of the underground Bund in Warsaw under Nazi occupation.

[Page 82]

One of the resolutions was to create workers' kitchens in all locations of the trade unions and establish tea-halls there. This was done not only to help the workers but to ensure that they would not become widely scattered. The resolution was implemented immediately and facilitated the widespread activity of the underground Bund.

Artur was also a member of the first Warsaw committee of the underground Bund. The other committee members were Engineer Avrom Blum (Abrasha), Luzer Klog, Sonia Novogrudska, Viktor Shulman, Bernard Goldshteyn, Tsluva Krishtal, and Yisocher Aykhenboym (Oskar). Only one, Bernard Goldshteyn, continued his leadership position for the full five years. Zygielbojm later wrote about Bernard, describing him as the bravest man he had ever known. After the uprising of the Warsaw Ghetto, in 1943, Avrom Blum was arrested by the Gestapo, and was murdered while in their custody. Luzer Klog was murdered during the Warsaw Ghetto uprising. Sonia Novogrudska was murdered in the gas chambers of Treblinka. Yisocher Aykhenboym later fought the Nazis in Italy with the Polish army. The veteran Bundist Viktor Shulman found his way to America, and Tsluva Krishtal went to China.

One of the functions that the underground Bund entrusted to Zygielbojm was work in the Jewish community. Zygielbojm, as a hostage, had already been legitimized as a Jewish leader of workers. He was now given another responsibility that required legitimacy: representing the Bund in the new Judenrat that had been established by the German occupation authorities.[11]

An unforgettable occasion was one of his appearances at a meeting of the Jewish community council. In the very first weeks after the fall of the city, the Germans wanted to enclose the Jews in a ghetto. They required the community itself to implement this.

During the few days when the community's leaders were discussing the creation of a ghetto, Zygielbojm was fervently opposed to the idea. Fearing that refusing this order would cause new problems for the community, the majority resolved to carry it out. The moment the resolution was adopted by the community's leadership, Zygielbojm declared as follows:

"This has been a historical resolution. Apparently, I was not strong enough to convince you that we must not do it. But my moral strength will not allow me to participate. I feel that I would lose the right to continue living if the Ghetto was created and I would survive

[Page 83]

unharmed. I therefore declare that I am renouncing my position. I know it is the chairman's duty to inform the Gestapo immediately of my resignation, and I am aware of the personal consequences that might follow. But I cannot do otherwise."

This declaration had an enormous effect. Fear receded, and people felt their moral responsibility for the importance of the Jews and their fate. The community council's resolution was annulled, and the debate whether the community should carry out the Gestapo's order concerning the ghetto began anew, in a very grave atmosphere. A compromise proposal was now adopted, as follows: the community council would not carry out the decree but would send messengers to tell the Jews about the order, so that they would be able to leave homes that would be excluded from the Ghetto.

The morning after the Warsaw Jewish community learned about the order, thousands came to the community building on Grzybowska Street and waited for concrete information on whether they had to leave homes that were not within the area designated for the ghetto. Zygielbojm talked to a crowd of over ten thousand Jews, calling on them to be courageous and stay in their homes until they would be forced out. The crowd dispersed with the resolve to refuse the order to enter the ghetto.

The talk on the street, as well as the resolution by the Jewish community council, did not go unnoticed by the Gestapo. Zygielbojm was summoned by the Gestapo and told to appear the next day, as the representative of the Jewish workers, to talk about important affairs.

The meaning of the invitation was clear. Naturally, Zygielbojm did not go, and from then on was not seen in public. The Gestapo strengthened its resolve to arrest him, regardless of the cost. There were indications that he was being spied on.

Considering these developments, the leadership of the underground Bund decided that it would be better for Zygielbojm to leave Poland. He was now entrusted with a special mission: informing the world about the atrocities the Germans were perpetrating towards the Jews. Although the escape route from Poland was dangerous, and the chances of success were slim, Zygielbojm set out, and overcame considerable difficulties to fulfill his mission.

[Page 84]

At an international forum, Shmuel Mordkhe Zygielbojm addressed a session of the Executive Committee of the Socialist Workers International and described the actions of the Nazis in Poland and towards the Jews in particular. His report made a huge impression. For the first time, the free world heard an authentic report from the locked, tortured, and murderous land that the Nazis had made of Poland.

The impression of this report, made in the first weeks of 1940, was described by D. Abramovitsh in the *Forverts* of New York:

"Here in Brussels, a few weeks before the invasion and ten days before the invasion of Norway, several dozen delegates of Social-Democratic parties in Europe assembled to consider the problems caused by the war.[12] Unexpectedly, among them was a man from a different planet. Speaking plainly, almost calmly, he painted a picture of a country under Nazi occupation. The horror and outrageousness of this war was in complete contrast to the positive, calm atmosphere of Brussels at the time. The listeners were shaken to the core."

"The people of Europe find themselves in a new world, one they never imagined, as they ignored all the press reports. They discovered the entire truth of the facts as reported by Artur, although human imagination refused to believe such terrible things. One can say that Artur was the conduit for the truth of the war, revealed for the first time as actual experiences, to the workers of Europe."

"From that moment on, Artur became a respected figure in the international Socialist movement."

After six weeks in Belgium and four weeks in France, where he experienced the military catastrophe of the Allies in 1940, Zygielbojm reached New York on September 12 of that year.

In the United States as well, Zygielbojm acquainted the public with the horrific actions of the Nazis in Poland. He traveled through the country under the auspices of the Jewish Labor Committee and informed his listeners about the scale of the torture and horror. In 1940 and 1941, the *Forverts* also published a series of his reports informing the Jews of America of the bitter fate that had overtaken their brethren across the sea.

[Page 85]

Artur briefly worked in a New York garment factory as a machine operator and then became the manager of the monthly *Di Tsukunft*. However, his heart and soul were on the streets of Warsaw and Lodz, Cracow and Lublin. Despite his limited mandate, he did what he could for the Jews of Poland. He was an active member of the American Bund office in Poland; at that time, the American Bund had already begun to receive information from the underground Bund about the terrible fate of the Jews in the ghettos.

He, who had witnessed the savage murderousness of the Nazis, was the person best equipped to understand the information that trickled in. He felt the pain of Jewish hearts, and identified with the tenacity of the brave underground fighters; after all, he had been one of them. On several occasions, he emphasized the courage and heroism of the Jews under Nazi occupation, especially of those Jews who were fighters. Describing the calamities of the first months of German rule, he noted:

"In addition to all this, one must be amazed at the fortitude and pride with which the Jews of Poland bore their unimaginable suffering."

Writing about the activities of the Jewish Labor movement, he notes:

"The secret emissaries who volunteered to risk their lives in order to help others manifested to the entire Jewish population extreme idealism, readiness for sacrifice, and courage. Their example had a tremendous effect; people found it easier to bear their own suffering."

Zygielbojm lived in London from the spring of 1942 to the spring of 1943. He went there on the important mission of representing the underground Bund of Poland in the Polish Parliament-in-exile.

This body already included a Jewish delegate, who represented all the Jewish political parties except the Bund. Zygielbojm immediately took a different stance than that of the previous Jewish delegates. Agreeing with the position of the underground Bund of Poland, as well as of the U.S. Bund representative, Zygielbojm recognized the Polish government-in-exile as the legitimate representative of Poland. However, he opposed it, both because of its composition (it included reactionary figures) and because of its political stance towards the Jews. He expressed his positions in his speeches as well as in his votes. Zygielbojm was the only deputy in the Polish National Council who did not support the government budgets.

In his speeches in the National Council, he touched on general national

[Page 86]

issues, bearing in mind the interests of the working classes and fighting for democratization. He made passionate demands to aid the Jewish population that was languishing in the ghettos and being tortured and murdered by the Nazi sadists.

He called for action by the government-in-exile regarding the murder of Jews. Artur intervened with Premier General Władysław Sikorski and with Interior Minister Stanisław Mikołajczyk. He also did so at the meetings of the National Council, where he ceaselessly demanded, asked, aroused, and presented practical suggestions. For example, he presented

Memorial Book of the Martyrs of Krasnystaw

the following three suggestions at a meeting of the National Council at the end of November, 1942:

> 1. The National Council demands that the government immediately require the Allies, except for the United States and England, to develop a plan to retaliate against German citizens, in order to force them to stop the murders of Jews.
> 2. The government shall take action to air-drop precise information, in German, about the murders of Jews, throughout Germany.
> 3. The government shall take steps to convene, as soon as possible, a special conference of the Allied governments, in order to initiate a public protest of all the nations attacked and a strong warning to the German people and their government.

In order to set these steps in motion, Zygielbojm conferred with Polish Foreign Minister Raczyński. However, the three demands were refused by the deciding countries of the Allied powers.[13]

Zygielbojm ceaselessly fore-grounded the tragedy of the Jews in the ghettos and camps. He did so not only in the arena of the Polish government-in-exile, but also for the British public. He was able to present his information concerning Poland in London's most influential newspapers and demanded that they publish the news of the horrors. This was one of his most difficult tasks, as he encountered strong refusals and disbelief. He was luckier with his efforts to bring the grim situation of the Jews before the British Labor Party and the representatives of other European Socialist parties. He presented his tragic information from the underground Bund at many mass rallies and conferences. Artur also appeared at many meetings of Jewish institutions throughout England, and tried to be active in efforts to help to rescue the Jews of Europe.

[Page 87]

He considered his continued liaison with the Jews of Poland to be his most sacred mission, as it enabled him to send help and important information, as well as giving the caged Jews the chance to tell the world about their needs and suffering, and the dangers they faced. The liaison was created with the help of the government-in-exile. The Jewish Labor committee of the United States sent large sums of money through these underground channels. Once the money arrived in Poland, it was directed towards helping Jews to continue their underground fight against the Nazis and purchase protective gear and weapons. The underground Bund also sent out reports about the murders of Jews, the gas chambers, and other calamities. For a long time, these reports were the only call for help from the Jews of Poland that reached the outside world. Thanks to them, people discovered what Hitler's murder machine was actually doing to the Jews of Europe.

On the other hand, Zygielbojm attempted to contact his suffering brothers and sisters. He did not do this only by means of letters delivered thorough underground channels, but over the radio as well: the words he said in London reached the Jews in Poland. They were heard in secret by special listeners, and their content was spread by word of mouth. His people, who were mourning their nearest and dearest as they awaited their own gruesome fate, heard words of comfort, cheer, and hope.

He worked in London feverishly for a year. His life was dictated by the obsession to help, help, help. What would work to stop the murdering hands? How could he break through the indifference of the world at large? Just as day cannot be distinguished from night in the far northern latitudes, so Artur did not distinguish waking from sleeping. One thought constantly gnawed at him: how to help them? The reports from home continued: the ghettos were less crowded, their number was declining, and the camps were being emptied. Zygielbojm was troubled: The Polish Jews, whose mouthpiece he was, were becoming fewer. Their original number of three and a half million had dwindled to several hundreds of thousands. The death operation continued twenty-four hours a day. The mind of Artur, that indefatigable fighter, felt doubt, and there was a pain in his heart. The darkness and death of Treblinka blazed in his mind. His mood was tinged with the breath of death.

His letter of April 30, 1943, to the American representative of the Bund in Poland, contains his report of a telegram that he had received

[Page 88]

from the underground Bund through secret channels. Artur writes, "This telegram breathes the knowledge that *everything* is ending... The information rules out any kind of work, even life itself."

The letters he wrote in his last days to his friends and comrades contain several thoughts and expressions of feeling. A letter to his younger brother in Johannesburg, South Africa, states, "I'm down to my last bits of strength, not because the work is hard but because of the unbearable helplessness. The reports from home are more terrible each day. I am tormented by the thought that I had been one of them – what right did I have to save myself? Why did I not share the common fate? I don't even have the relief of thinking that my work helped to save someone from the pitiless sword of extermination."

As we know, the spring of 1943 was not the first time Zygielbojm had confronted the problem of death. During the years of World War II, this activist of the Jewish Labor movement had been in situations where he had to balance honor, life, and death.

During the very first weeks of the Nazi regime in Warsaw, Zygielbojm declared, in a Judenrat meeting, "I feel I would have no right to go on living if the Ghetto is established and I would not be affected."

Zygielbojm had already decided that he would sacrifice himself in the struggle for honor, and the life of the Jewish population. That gave him the confidence and courage that he needed as a representative of the people. It was he who wrote about the early period of the Nazi reign of terror in Poland: "Believe it or not, but absolute readiness to die confers superhuman strength to fight for life. This complete readiness for death, which has empowered me since my first day in Warsaw under Nazi rule, has now restored my calm and resolve."

There were difficult moments when he, who was ready to die, wanted to hasten the process. That was when he was thrust back from the Dutch border into the hands of the Gestapo. As Zygielbojm wrote, "For the first time in my life I thought about death as a savior. For the first time, I thought seriously about suicide." He continued, several hours later, "What's the worst that could happen? I'll die. Haven't I been ready for it for the past few months?"

[Page 89]

All this was when and where he could have been seized by the murderous claws of the Gestapo. But Artur Zygielbojm ended his life in a free part of the world. Previously, over there, his readiness to die gave him the peace of mind to continue living through the worst dangers. Now, over here, the prospect of life made him restless and ashamed to go on living.

Speaking over London Radio on July 2, 1943, this emissary of Jewish pain said, "Imagine the terrible disaster of methodically murdering an entire nation! Each of us who grasps the horror of the catastrophe must be seized by shame for still being alive… Anyone who does not do everything in his power to stop the mass murders assumes the moral responsibility for them… The mass graves that fill daily with thousands of Jewish women, children, and elderly persons are constant burning wounds that every decent person must feel as a pain and defilement that can happen to him."

When the Jews of Warsaw and Lublin were violated, Zygielbojm was violated in London. When the Jews of Lodz and Vilna were killed, he was killed in London. He was a small part of them, a slender thread in the large national web.

That intimate connection was so powerful that he declared, at a meeting in London in the Ohel Jewish center: "If the Jews of Poland are obliterated, I feel that I have no right to continue living."

The early readiness to die became transformed into a duty, and finally – an inevitable obligation. An emissary from the Polish underground organization arrived in London, with a special message from the Jewish delegates (including the Bund delegate). The emissary, Jan Karski, passed him the following message that the Jewish delegates in Poland wanted to transmit to the Jewish leaders in the free world: "Let them go to all the major British and American departments and agencies. Tell them to stay there until they have guarantees that they are working on a way to save the

Jews. Let them not eat or drink but slowly expire before the eyes of an indifferent world. Let them die. Maybe that will shake the conscience of the world."

Zygielbojm's response was: "Mr. Karski, I myself will do everything I can to help them. Everything! I will do whatever they ask, if I am only given the chance."

During his year in London, Zygielbojm explored all the possibilities, but nothing resulted in rescue for the millions of victims. The emissary from Poland suggested

[Page 90]

a new "way." This was actually a request and demand of the leading speaker for the murdered Jews: Die, on the chance that it might 'shake the conscience of the world.' Shmuel Mordkhe Zygielbojm, the working youth from Krasnystaw, the Labor activist of Warsaw, the delegate of the Polish Jews to the free world, was fully prepared to carry out the order that the leaders of the murdered Jews had sent from the vale of tears. He was the only one who fulfilled the order that the Jewish ghetto leaders directed towards the Jewish leaders of the free world. He was the only one to make the ultimate sacrifice. On the night of May 11-12, he ended his own life.

His death made a powerful impression far and wide. It was marked by hundreds of newspapers and magazines in many countries. The words of his last will and testament were noted by the U.S. Congress and made their way through press and radio to all the countries of the world. For a while, their indifference cracked, and they were ashamed. Their consciences were shaken for a moment. The voluntary suicide of this one person agitated the remnants of the Jewish survivors in Poland, those who had witnessed the mass murder of their nearest and dearest while awaiting their own demise. A report by the underground Bund in Poland, on May 24, 1944, described Zygielbojm's suicide as a heroic act. Jewish workers in Warsaw, Lodz, and the labor camps assembled in secret and honored his memory with a few quiet words.

Thus did Shmuel Mordkhe Zygielbojm live with his people, and die for them.

Translator's footnotes:

1. The first and middle names have been transcribed from Yiddish, and the last name is presented in Polish, to conform to the Polish spelling. He was known by his alias as Artur, which was sometimes spelled Arthur.
2. The groschen was then the smallest unit of currency.
3. An allusion to Genesis 41:53, which prophesies seven years of scarcity in Egypt following seven years of plenty.
4. This was the notorious "Beilis Affair" (1913) in which the Jewish Menachem Mendel Beilis was accused of the ritual murder of a Christian child.
5. This reference is obscure.
6. "Workers' homes" were a system of low-cost housing for workers.
7. This was most likely *Di Algemeyne Entsiklopedye* (*The General Encyclopedia*) a Yiddish language publishing project created in Berlin, Paris, and New York from 1932 to 1966.
8. "Endeks" was the acronym of the National Democrats (N. D.), a fascist anti-Semitic political party that was active from the late 19th century to the German invasion of 1939.
9. Zygmunt Zaremba was an important Polish Socialist activist and publicist.
10. *Folks-Tsaytung* translates as "people's newspaper."
11. A Judenrat (Jewish council) was an administrative body established in German-occupied Europe during World War II which purported to represent a Jewish community in dealings with the Nazi authorities.
12. Belgium was invaded by Germany on May 10, 1940. Norway was invaded on April 9.
13. The writer seems to be very careful here, which renders the actual meaning unclear.

Original footnote:

a. Zygielbojm had a son and a daughter with his first wife. His second wife, the dramatic artist Manya Rozen, bore him a son. Manya, who was active in the underground Bund, was murdered with their son Artur Tevye, probably during the Warsaw Ghetto uprising, at about the same time as the adult Artur. In any case, Artur did not know of their deaths. His first wife, Golda, and their daughter Rivka, both of whom lived in the Warsaw Ghetto, shared in the fate of almost all the Jews of Poland. Only the oldest son, Yoysef Leyb, lived to see the end of the war.

[Page 91]

Ben Tsukerman
(Memories of a Boyhood Friend)

L. Grinberg, Winnipeg, Canada

Ben Tsukerman
(Chairman of the Krasnystaw Natives' Committee,
Los Angeles)

Whenever I want to refresh my memories of my hometown, Krasnystaw (Lublin Province, Poland), of 40-45 years ago, I first think of our Study House, where I spent much of my time, and from which I gained all it could provide. I remember my

[Page 92]

friends in the Study House, who were the best friends I could have. I especially remember my friend Berl, or Benny, as he is now known in his new hometown.

Berl was remarkable for his pointed witticisms, shrewd intellectual conversation, strong character, and great courage.

His courage and sarcastic remarks were very helpful to us later, during our "Enlightenment" period, when we were persecuted by the community. I would like to mention a few episodes.

This was how Berl addressed one of our learned attackers, who were very learned, before a large crowd.

"It looks as though you're planning to lord it over us very soon." When the person asked him how he had come to that conclusion, he said, "The Talmud explicitly states, 'Anyone who distresses Israel will become a chief,' and you are lording it over us like Haman the wicked did over the Jews."[1] The man was silenced, and said nothing more against the Study House crowd. Another insolent man, who was far from learned, was countered by Berl as follows: "First, sit on the study bench for ten or twelve years, and be studious. Only then might you be entitled to speak against the Study House men."

This was how Ben silenced the hypocrites and all those who enjoyed belittling others.

* * *

The Study House became too confining. People searched for new paths and new ways of thinking. Popular options were Zionism, Tze'irei Tziyon, and, later, Poalei Tziyon.[2] Berl was the most active everywhere. Yet he always remembered those of his friends who were in need, and often took them to his home for a meal; his parents had created a warm and welcoming environment.

* * *

During conscription to the army, Berl was drafted, but felt that he could not be part of the Czarist forces. Parting with him was painful, especially the very last goodbyes, which were rich in hope and heartfelt wishes.[3]

* * *

Once in New York, Berl found that he was not suited for work in sweatshops, peddling, insurance, and many other occupations. After several years of struggling to make a living, Berl and his family – wife and child – found their way to western Canada. Like many other idealists, he planned to become a farmer.

[Page 93]

He settled on a farm in the remotest part of the wilderness, where the government provided free land, subject to certain conditions. It was located miles away from the nearest farmer or any town – roughly thirty miles–and conditions were unbelievably primitive. He struggled stubbornly for several years and relinquished the farm only when the health of his entire family became threatened. He moved to Saskatoon in the Province of Saskatchewan.

Benny was able to make a living in Saskatoon and deserved to rest after each day's work. But how could he rest, when the few Jews who were there experienced no traces of a Jewish life? He soon began agitating tirelessly for a synagogue, a Talmud-Torah, and other components necessary to maintain Jewish culture.[4] He put great effort into this project, though he himself was a radical. Before long, a synagogue was built as well as a Talmud-Torah for children. A ritual slaughterer, who doubled as cantor, was brought in, as well as two good teachers.[5] Thanks to these institutions, the Jews of Saskatoon began to live as Jews, and strove to excel. Everyone in the community became active, and people were interested in holding responsible positions (unpaid). Thus, everyone was active, and Benny was happy.

Yet he was still not satisfied. After much effort, he established a local branch of the Poalei-Tziyon movement. His enthusiasm influenced others, who had previously avoided community activity out of principle, to become participants. People who had been fervent anarchists and Bundists joined Poalei-Tziyon. A culture of national, cultural, and political activity came into being. People began to spend their evenings and free days in the library created by the Poalei-Tziyon club. People were busy reading, entering into discussions, and becoming intellectually stimulated.

As a young boy, Berl began to be interested in the Bible as well as in Talmudic discussions. He loved Hebrew and Hebrew literature. At age 17 or 18, he published an article in the Hebrew weekly *Ha-Kol*, in the form of a letter. It was a response to the rich, Polish Hassidic hypocrites, whose newspapers published complaints that religious studies were doomed, basing themselves on the Talmudic precept that "Torah will issue forth from the poor."[6] Over half of the poor young Jewish men in Poland had begun to abandon their religious studies in favor of learning a trade, or gaining a general European education. This was true of city Jews as well. They were all thinking in practical terms. In his response, Berl pointed out the hypocrisy of the rich Hassids: they married their daughters to rich professionals rather than to poor religious students. Several of these families had sons-in-law who were chemists, engineers, and lawyers. Berl's response made a great impression, as he was exposing actual aspects of community life.

* * *

[Page 94]

In 1918, at the end of World War I, Benny left everything and hurried to Europe to save his parents and the eight children who remained at home (they were a family of twelve).

He was literally one of the first people from the American continent to visit Poland at that time. Traveling to Europe was very difficult. Passenger ships carried limited numbers of people, and only as far as London. At that time, it was impossible to buy any travel tickets directly to Warsaw, but –

if one pulled the right strings – a ticket to Paris could be bought. Once in Paris, it became clear that it was impossible to go to Warsaw, because the trains were almost exclusively for diplomats. Special train cars were earmarked for people such as the extremely wealthy, well-known bankers, and internationally famous manufacturers. Ordinary people could not travel. Getting a travel permit could take as long as three or four months. However, Benny contacted highly placed people, one of whom was an important Canadian diplomat. Thanks to his logical approach and personal appeal – or luck – Benny received permission to travel on the diplomats' train. Thus, he was literally one of the first ten passengers to arrive from America.

I will not linger on the various welcomes that were arranged for him, or the mood of celebration that overtook the town when he came. I heard about these in Warsaw, where I was living at the time. Let me just present a small example of an example of Benny's work, not for any reward but out of innate kindness and courtesy.

Achieving his goal – bringing his family out of Europe – met with many difficulties. Two of the four boys (they had been six altogether) were over 18, and the new Polish government did not allow them to leave the country. But Benny would not leave them behind. The new Polish government had no policy regarding emigration at that time. Even the shipping companies were not in touch with the government about carrying emigrants. But Benny let nothing stop him. He sent cables to Ottawa, London, and to every other location that might help. Finally, after unimaginable efforts, Benny received permission, along with all the required documentation, visas, etc., for his entire family of ten.

This was followed, naturally, by requests from relatives, friends, and acquaintances for help from Benny to leave Poland. These requests were accompanied by tears and entreaties, as the process was fraught with danger.

[Page 95]

Letting people know the truth, that help was impossible, was useless; he promised to do his best once he was back in Canada. He did explore every avenue while still in Poland. He selected some of those who were worthiest of his aid. By various means, ideas, connections, etc., he was able to take several young men with him. He swore solemnly that as soon as he came home, he would do everything in his power to get them out of Poland.

Benny returned to Canada. While looking for a new job, he also sought rich, compassionate people who would help him to bring over these people who had suffered during the war. He was able to collect funds (I don't know the amount) and buy passage, as well as sending people money to cover expenses. Benny knew which cases were the most urgent. I had to wait until February 1921. It was a long wait, but I knew that my turn would come. I received my ticket, affidavit, and fifty dollars for expenses. I arrived in Canada at the end of May, 1921. Three years later, I was able to bring over my wife and three children, with no help from anyone. I was one of the sixth group of ten people that Benny's compassion helped to bring to America, without their families. The families were all brought over later, thanks to the efforts of husbands and sons.

And every time we natives of Krasnystaw gathered, we spoke mainly of Benny's great compassion. We always said, "If not for Benny, where would we be?"

[Page 96]

[Blank]

Translator's footnotes:

1. The Talmud quote, from Tractate Gittin 56b, projects the fate of the biblical Haman for the harasser: Haman was hung from a gallows (Esther 7:10). Commentators see this as an expression of God's status: God can do battle only with great chiefs.
2. Tzei'rei Tziyon (Young People of Zion) was a Labor Zionist youth movement in Eastern Europe in the early 20th century. Poalei Tziyon (Workers of Zion) was a movement of Marxist-Zionist workers founded in European cities around the turn of the same century.
3. To avoid conscription he departed Krasnystaw and traveled to New York.
4. A Talmud-Torah (Yid. Talmud Toyre) is an elementary religious school for boys.

5. The ritual slaughter (Hebrew: Shochet) or kosher butcher is a person officially certified as competent to prepare cattle and poultry in the manner prescribed by Jewish law.
6. A quote from Tractate Nedarim 81a.

[Page 97]

The Destruction of Krasnystaw

[Page 98]

[Blank]

[Page 99]

The Extermination
(A Witness Statement)

by Aryeh Shtuntsayger

The Jews of Krasnystaw began to be "resettled" during Passover in 1942. On May 11, 1942, most of the town's Jews were taken to Belzec, where they were gruesomely murdered in the crematoriums. It was the 22 day of Iyyar, a date that is now the annual memorial day for the Jews of Krasnystaw.[1] But the extermination of the Krasnystaw Jews actually began much earlier.

On September 14, 1939, about two weeks after the German invasion of Poland, the invading army neared Krasnystaw. The battle for the town lasted three hours. The Polish army retreated to the hills in the east, from which they defended the town against the invaders who attacked from the Lublin side. Bullets flew over the town. The population hid in cellars. All the Jews hid in one cellar, in terror, and heard the explosions outside. It grew silent on the third day. The Poles had vanished. It was afternoon when the dead streets of Krasnystaw were filled with the stomping of German army boots and the bestial yelling of their officers.

The first soldiers who entered the town immediately declared "war" on the civilian population. A lieutenant and the three soldiers with him used their rifle butts to break though the front door of Ben-Tziyon Halpern's house, where six Jewish families had found refuge in the cellar.

[Page 100]

Terrified to death, they did not know what to do, and decided not to open the door. The Germans battered the door, but it did not surrender. The Germans then went to Dobeh Ayzenberg's house, where seven Jewish families were hiding in the cellar. When the Germans tried to break down the door, the frightened Jews opened it themselves. The Germans took all the Jewish captives into the courtyard and separated the men from the women. One German handed out chocolates to the women and children, as the other soldiers took the men away.

Some of the Murdered Jewish Families of Krasnystaw

Mendl Binder with his wife and children

Among the men was sixty-year-old Leybl Kupershtok and Avrom-Mordkhe Shteyn with his fourteen-year-old son Hershele. The women looked at their departing men fearfully. A German told them, with a cruel smile, "They'll be brought back soon." The men, however, never returned.

[Page 101]

Two days later, Leyb the shoemaker, one of the men who had been taken away, suddenly appeared on the street. His tongue had been shot off and his face was bloody. Unable to speak, he led a few people to the cellar where all the men who had been taken lay, shot to death. Apparently, the Germans had taken all seven, one by one, to the cellar. At the entrance, each had been shot in the back of the neck (nape), and the body then dragged into the cellar. The German who had aimed at Leyb had not been entirely successful: the bullet struck him in the face and tore out his tongue. He had laid in the cellar, unconscious, for two days, regained consciousness on the third day and come out of the cellar. Two days later, Leyb died of his injuries.

Naturally, the town was shocked to hear of this. Some people tried to reassure themselves by saying that it had happened in the heat of battle. Others interpreted it as meaning that the Germans would not shoot everyone. However, they soon discovered how false this hope was.

Young Jews of Krasnystaw doing forced labor for the Germans

On the fourth day, the Poles resumed their fight. The Germans then stationed more than forty local Jews in an open field, as a buffer against the Polish army.

"Once you are shot, your bodies will protect us," argued one German.

During this "demonstration," a young man called Pinyeh Polkovnik was shot. The Jews were forced to dig his grave and bury him in the middle of the field.

[Page 102]

This was not the end of the bloody performance. The Germans took all the Jews to the river and placed them opposite a sergeant firing a machine gun. The officer ordered the sergeant to fire – one, two, three – but he did not. It was nothing but a ruse to terrorize the Jews. This recurred several times in different locations; each time, the group of forty Jews was placed opposite a machine gun. Finally, the officer ordered the Jews to run for home. As they began to run, they were shot in the legs. Some were badly injured.

Mendel Shok with his entire family
– one of the families that were murdered

Who knows whether any of the Krasnystaw Jews would have been able to escape the murderous hands of the Germans. Luckily, however, the Germans left the town after ten or eleven days, following an agreement with the U.S.S.R.

During those ten days, the Germans bullied and mistreated the town's Jews. First of all, they began to take Jews for forced labor.

[Page 103]

The Germans assigned them to the filthiest tasks, such as cleaning the town's toilet with their bare hands, etc. Later, a German officer defecated in a hat and set it on the head of a Jew.

Another group of Jews were burying a horse that had been shot to death. When one of the Jews was sickened at the thought of grabbing the horse by its bloody muzzle, a German officer struck him in the face with his whip, yelling, "It won't bite! Pick it up!" Once the horse was partly buried, the Jews had to pose with it while the German took a picture, apparently in order to send it to his "Gretchen" and demonstrate how he taught the Jews to work.

Once, when Jews were rounded up for work, the German found a Jew named Noteh Faygenboym carrying his tallis and tefillin.[2] The Germans tied him to a tree in a city park, where he stood all day. At twilight, the Jew Shoul-Leyb Birnboym was forced to carry Noteh, wrapped in his tallis, in a wheelbarrow through the town, shouting, "I am a Jew, I caused the war!"

The arrival of the Red Army in Krasnystaw spelled salvation for the Jews of the town. The general mood improved, as Jews quickly returned to their normal affairs. Unfortunately, the good spirits did not last for long, after rumors came that the Red Army was leaving, and the Germans were returning.

One of the murdered Jewish families: Henech Shok and his family

Several dozen Jews then fled to Wladimir-Wolynsk, across the Bug River, where the Soviets planned to stay permanently.

When the Germans arrived in Krasnystaw for the second time, they began attacking the town's Jews with true German zeal.

The Soviet retreat took three days. They finally stationed themselves not far from Lublin. The town was free of

[Page 104]

soldiers for two days. During those days, the Jews were in a state of terrible fear and insecurity. When the German military marched into town for the second time, they immediately began to snatch up Jews for forced labor. Jews were brutally dragged out of their homes and beaten severely. Beards were viciously cut. The Germans took the trouble to render the Jews hideous by cutting off half their beards or slashing their faces. This "task" was accompanied by ridicule, mockery, and murderous blows. Among the first victims were Yankev Langman, the ritual slaughterer, Yehoshu'a Vizenberg, Hersh Eydelsberg, and others. Motl Likhtenshteyn was singled out for special torture: he was badly beaten while his beard was being cut, and later had to pay money to be released. However, the Germans were not done with him: he was dragged out of his house every day and forced to pay money.

The major task of the Jews was rebuilding the bridge that the Poles had set on fire during their retreat.

The Krasnystaw Judenrat was established during that period; it was the decision of the Jews themselves.[3] The Germans were snatching up Jews at random. Anyone who had been caught once had to continue coming every morning, under threat of being shot. Apparently, the Jews sought a way to exchange those who had been picked up, and decided to elect a Judenrat, which would regulate the supply of Jews to the Germans for labor. It was set up by Lipeh Raykhman (Chairman), Yisokher Rozenboym, Alter Katz (Lipeh Raykhman's son-in-law) and Dovid Zilbertson. Others, such as Zaynvl Mitelman, served in the Judenrat later.

The Judenrat supplied Jews for daily work on the bridge. At first, people shared in the work schedule equally. Gradually, however, the rich began to hire the poor to take their places. Characteristically, though the Jews were beaten daily while at work, many hired themselves out to work instead of the rich, to get some money and avoid death by hunger. This situation continued for about four months. Afterwards, the Germans decided to use the Judenrat "properly."

One day, the Judenrat ordered all the Jews to bring all their gold, silver, and other valuables to the town elders' office. Those who withheld anything were threatened by death. At seven the next morning, the town was surrounded by German police to prevent Jews from escaping. Lipeh Raykhman stood at the large crate where everyone deposited their property. Then the Jews were severely whipped, and had to

[Page 105]

jump down the stairs in a single leap. Anyone who fell in the course of these "gymnastics" was beaten again and had to repeat the leap. The Jews were so terrified that most of them handed over everything they owned.

However, the Jews were not permitted to return home yet. They were driven into barracks for "delousing." Their beards were cut off, and they were beaten and tortured for the rest of the day. Finally, they had to clean the toilets of the barracks with their bare hands. They had to report for work the next day, when the torture was repeated.

Some time later, the Germans ordered the establishment of a Jewish police force. The community leaders made efforts to include their sons in the Jewish police, hoping to save them from other problems.

The police force consisted of Moyshe Shmaragd, Ben-Tziyon Rozenblat, Yoysef Zilberman, Zaynvl Mitelman, and others. Their station was at the house of Avigdor Feldman, near the marketplace. The mission of the police was to procure Jews for work and to obtain new contributions. This situation lasted all winter and through the end of the summer of 1940.

In the fall of 1940, the Germans demanded 60 Jews. These Jews were supposed to go and dig trenches in Belzec. At that time, no one knew that mass graves were being prepared for the Jews of the entire region. As no Jews wanted to report for this duty, the SS and the Jewish police snatched up Jews to be transported. Nochem Eydelberg, a witness to this event, was one of those taken.

The Jews were marched to Izbica.[4] They were beaten viciously and forced to run all the way, chased by German riders.

About ten thousand Jews from other towns had already been brought to the small town of Izbica, where they were packed into locked rail cars. SS soldiers and Ukrainians guarded the trains and administered terrible beatings.

The Jews were held in stables, under gruesome conditions. They were given no food; beatings and roll calls were routine. Many Jews were shot, and many more died as a result of torture. Dovid Burshtin (Yidl Nirnberg's son-in-law) of Krasnystaw was among the dead. The Jews from other towns suffered many more fatalities, as they were far from their homes and could receive no help. After two months of

[Page 106]

this labor, many of the Jews had died or been murdered. A new transport of Jews was brought from Krasnystaw and other towns. This period of terrible suffering lasted four months. The Krasnystaw Judenrat then ransomed the Jews from their town, using money collected from the Jewish community.

During the ransom process, the Germans often cheated, taking the money but continuing to hold the Jews. The Jews were finally released and came home by way of Zamość. However, the Germans began to snatch Jews up again the very next day, for work in Belzec.

A series of "resettlements" began in the early winter of 1940-1941.

Jews were now forbidden to live in Krasnystaw. They were relocated in Zakrzew[5], a small town not far away. Only the Judenrat and a few Jewish professionals who worked for Germans remained. These Jews were forced to live in the Grablie neighborhood, which was turned into a ghetto. Jews were prohibited from traveling.

At that time, the Krasnystaw district was governed by two SS villains, Ludwig and Engels. They spent hours riding their motorcycles, shooting every Jew they spotted. This was how Yehoshua Vizenberg was shot, as well as many other Jews who had arrived from other towns. The Jews had to clear away the corpses. Many Jews were similarly murdered in the other towns to which they had been driven. The brothers Efrayim and Fishl Listhoyz were killed in this manner, in Żółkiew.[6]

In the spring of 1941, the Germans were preparing for war with the U.S.S.R. Large forces of the German army marched through Krasnystaw to the Soviet borders. Conditions grew even worse for the Jews. An SS group stationed in the town conscripted Jews for work every day. The Jews had to do everything for the soldiers who passed through. They were badly beaten. The poorest Jews, as well as those who had been brought from other towns, suffered the most. Hunger and need were so great that in spite of the horrific conditions, many Jews hired themselves out to richer Jews in order to take their place at forced labor.[7]

The war with the U.S.S.R. started on June 22. Endless German army units streamed to the front. The Jews, whose lives hadn't counted for much until then, now became completely up for grabs. Any soldier could do whatever he wanted to the Jews. Every atrocity was justified by the claim that they had provoked the war.

[Page 107]

The town's main Study House was demolished and desecrated. The books were incinerated or ripped up. Although the Study House in Grablie was still intact, no Jews went to pray there, due to fear of encountering Germans, which would mean certain death. The German soldiers often came to Grablie to inspect the ghetto and had turned the Study House into a place to "meet" women.

Russian prisoners began to arrive. The Ukrainian prisoners were released, but the Russian and Jewish prisoners continued to be held without food, and thousands of them died.

On Simchat Torah 1941, a small group of Jews gathered at Mates Faygenboym's home for community prayer.[8] Stepanski, a volksdeutscher, came in with Judenrat chairman Lipeh Raykhman and his helper, Yisro'el Rozenboym, and dragged out Jews to help bury dead Russian prisoners.[9] One of this group was the survivor Nokhem Aydelberg, who reported that he was taken, along with the group, to the horse market for the purpose of digging a mass grave there for the prisoners. When they began to take out the corpses, they found many still alive. Initially, the Jews did not want to remove those who were alive, but the Germans beat them savagely and forced them to bury the living prisoners, who included many Jews. When the "living" prisoners were being taken, many of them clamped onto the grass. As they were still conscious, they used their last shreds of strength to defend themselves. The burial party was whipped and forced to stamp on the unfortunate prisoners in order to create space for additional burials. It was a gruesome scene, beyond anyone's wildest imaginings.

Many of the freed Ukrainian prisoners, as well as Russians, formed partisan groups.

Memorial Book of the Martyrs of Krasnystaw

The grueling, nightmarish winter of 1942 began. The "resettlement" of Krasnystaw's Jews started on the seventh day of Passover.[10] About 60 Jewish families were then living in Grablie, most of them originally from other locations. The remaining Jews of Krasnystaw had already died or been murdered.

At about noon that day, the Grablie area was encircled by Ukrainians, and German Sonderdienst, gendarmes, and SS forces.[11] All the Jews were assembled within 30 minutes. People grabbed whatever they could and brought their small bundles with them. They were taken to the village of Izbica, where all the Jews of the vicinity were gathered.

Many were shot en route. Among them were

[Page 108]

Borech-Hersh Luft, and Motl Likhtenshteyn's wife. The other Krasnystaw Jews, along with thousands of other Jews, were hauled to Belzec, where they were murdered and incinerated. This operation ended on May 12.

May 12 marked the tragic end of Jewish life in Krasnystaw. Only a few remained in the town. Some who had managed to hide later received permits to work for the SS, and some were permitted to go on living as professionals. A bit later, some Jews arrived from various locations and were able to hide.

The only survivors of Krasnystaw's Jewish community were Yekl Kershenboym, the military tailor; Yisro'el Taytlboym, the locksmith; and Shayndl Shok, the seamstress. Others who were able to survive in hiding were Mates Shok, Nechemiya Shtuntsayger and his daughter Rivka, Yankev Kenobl. Zelik Binder, Mayer Faygnboym, and the brothers Nokhem and Moyshe Eydelberg. Other survivors were the Judenrat members Lipeh Raykhman and Dovid Boymfeld. Jews who worked for Germans continued to do so for some time.

During that period, Krasnystaw was on the route of German Jews going to the Belzec death camp. They had to leave their belongings in Krasnystaw. The few remaining Jews had to sort these clothes; this work was unpaid. They made do by stealing objects from the goods they were sorting, and exchanging these objects with non-Jews in return for food. From time to time, the Germans brought Jewish women to Krasnystaw, defined them as "girlfriends," and arranged work for them.

This was the case with the German named Bauer, who was the deputy town elder. He brought two young Jewish sisters, one of whom was very beautiful. He put them to work at the town bathhouse. The more beautiful sister was his "girlfriend." After enjoying her for two months, he sent two gendarmes to take the girls away and shoot them.

In the course of several months, the following Jews were shot under varying circumstances: Sheyndl Shok, Nechemiya Shtuntsayger, his daughter Rivka, Yekl Kenobl, Zelik Binder, Mayer Faygnboym, and others.

In September of 1942, the last Jews of Krasnystaw were taken to Belzec, and some were sent to the Trawniki concentration camp.[12]

Thus ended the horrific tragedy of the Jews of Krasnystaw, along with all the Jews of Poland, Germany, and the other countries that were taken by

[Page 109]

the murderous German forces. It was a disaster of unimaginable proportions that was impossible to delineate. No language had the vocabulary to describe the fearful crimes and torture that the Jews of the occupied countries suffered at the bloody hands of Hitler's savages.

Let these few words brand an eternal mark of Cain, and permanent shame, on the bloodthirsty German people. Let the blood of the innocent victims continue seething, and demand revenge. Let the Jewish people remember their martyrs forever, and may their memory reinforce the struggle to bring every single Jew out of exile, into his own free country – Israel.

Memorial Book of the Martyrs of Krasnystaw

Translator's footnotes:

1. The date of 22 Iyyar 5702 on the Hebrew calendar corresponds to 9 May 1942. The 24th corresponds to 11 May 1942.
2. A tallis (or tallit) is a prayer shawl with a ritually knotted fringe at each corner. Tefillin, or phylacteries, are a set of small black leather boxes with leather straps containing scrolls of parchment inscribed with verses from the Torah. Observant adult Jews wear both a tallis and tefillin during weekday and Sunday morning prayers.
3. A Judenrat (literally 'Jewish council') was an administrative body established in German-occupied Europe during World War II, to represent a Jewish community in dealings with the Nazi authorities.
4. Izbica is located about 12 km south of Krasnystaw on the road to Zamość.
5. Zakrzew is located about 40 km south of Lublin and about 55 km west-northwest of Zamość.
6. Żółkiew is located about 30 km west-southwest of Krasnystaw.
7. This sentence has been retained, although it is redundant.
8. October 13, 1941.
9. Volksdeutsche was the Nazi German term for people whose language and culture had German origins but who did not hold German citizenship.
10. April 8.
11. Sonderdienst were Nazi paramilitary formations created in the Nazi-occupied areas.
12. The Trawniki Concentration Camp was located about 22 km north-northwest of Krasnystaw.

[Page 110]

In Sacred Memory

by Mordechai Futerman

When I heard that a Yizkor-Book for the martyrs was being prepared, I decided to add a brick to the monument commemorating our holy fathers, mothers, sisters, brothers, relatives, and acquaintances, who were gruesomely murdered by the bloodthirsty German beasts in human form.

The regional capital of Krasnystaw lies 52 km southeast of Lublin. Until 1939, the town's population was about 15,000, 2,000 of which were

Jews. It was ringed by gardens, and made a wonderful impression on first-time visitors.

The roughly 10,000 non-Jews of the town were not too friendly to the resident Jews. They were ruled by a type of restrained anti-Semitism, but there were never overt anti-Semitic acts. For this reason, no one had ever even dreamed of the horrible disaster that drew near, from the first few shots at the Polish-German border. True, people had a vague feeling of unrest, but no one could have imagined the way in which it would begin, and how it would end.

The wholesale destruction of the Jewish population began shortly after the first German troops marched into Krasnystaw.

[Page 111]

Jews of various ages and occupations began to be brought out of one of the houses in the center of town, on the pretext that they had shot at the German soldiers. They were taken to the entrance to one of the cellars in that building, and each was shot in the back of the neck. They fell, one by one, on top of each other, into the cellar.

Among the Jews murdered that day were the leather merchant Leybl Kupershtok (Leybl, Koyftshe's son), a Hassid in his sixties, and his son-in-law Mendele Zilberaykh; the textile merchant Avrom-Mordkhe Shteyn (Ben-Tziyon Halpern's son-in-law, in his forties); Leyb Blumshteyn the shoemaker (Leyb Binyomeles, in his late thirties); Yehoshu'a Katz the tailor's apprentice (in his late twenties), and four others. The German gangsters allowed these men to be buried only three days later.[1]

It was horrible to find out later, after people had gone into the cellar, that three of those who had been shot showed signs of life. When they were brought to the hospital the doctor declared that there stood no chance of surviving, due to loss of blood. And indeed, they surrendered their sacred souls to God two days later.

That same day, forty Jews were driven out of town, to a location close to the German army positions. The Jews were held for twenty-four hour without food or drink. After their release they walked back home through the fields, when a German rascal decided to "have fun." He shot Pinches Berman the tailor (Pinyeh Yisro'el, Itshe's son). The same rascal ordered two Jews to dig a pit and place the recently shot man in it. When they noticed that the man was still alive, the terrible murderer remarked, "But of course – he's a Jew, after all." The unfortunate Pinyeh was thus buried alive.

It is worth noting that this gory task was carried out not by the bloodthirsty Gestapo or the S.S., but by the "more refined" officers and soldiers of the regular army.

This was the blood-soaked prologue to the even more brutal drama that overtook our nearest and dearest.

Eight days later, it became possible for Jews to flee to the Soviet side, across the Bug River. The river was about ninety kilometers from Krasnystaw. The way was open, and people were free to go. Unfortunately, not everyone took advantage of this opportunity, as they did not yet grasp the full extent of the danger.

[Page 112]

People took pains to explain that the events of eight days earlier could not recur, that it had occurred in the heat of the battles between the Polish and the German armies that were still ongoing. Jews reassured themselves that the future would be more peaceful.

Who could have persuaded a man like Zaynvl the blacksmith to leave his forge, where he had labored day and night for years, serving the population of the entire province with his own hands. Everyone, Jews and Gentiles alike, knew Zaynvl. No one else in the province could shoe a horse like he did. The worst anti-Semites would come to him, and Zaynvl responded. His workday began at 2:00 or 3:00 a.m. and lasted until sundown, winter and summer alike. He never took time off, except, of course, for Shabbat and Jewish holidays.

On Shabbat and on holidays he would go to the Grablie Study House, the closest to his home. Every holiday before prayers began, one could see Zaynvl surrounded by people who listened to his tales of serving in the

Czarist army, and his participation – along with his three brothers – in World War I (1914-1918). He would also tell interesting stories that he had heard from his father about his compulsory 25 years of service as a "Cantonist" in the Czarist army.[2]

This was the life of Zaynvl Goldberg, the Jewish blacksmith, of Krasnystaw, where he and his family lived. The family consisted of wife and six children – four sons and two daughters, one of whom now lives in Brazil. He was happy, industrious, and decent. His children were raised in the same spirit of love for work, a family characteristic.

This was the case until the blood-soaked German invasion of Poland, when the German specter of death began rampaging through the cities and towns of Poland and did not spare Zaynvl the blacksmith and his family.

Unfortunately, there were no surviving witnesses to the last hours of Zaynvl and his family. Everyone knew that they did not fear the hands or weapon of any Gentile, and that they would not perish in any revolt. If this did occur, and Zaynvl and his family were killed in the course of a revolt, it could only be the result of the murderers' use of the "refined" methods they had learned over the years from their gangster teachers.

[Page 113]

Now, the forge, in its beautiful wooden structure, built near the Lublin-Zamosć road with the sweat and blood of the Jewish Zaynvl Goldberg, is held by Gentiles, perhaps even by the neighbors who lived peacefully with him before the horrible war but looked calmly on when "their Zaynvl" was driven away into a death camp with his family, enabling his "good neighbors" to take the property that he accumulated through his hard work. Perhaps they didn't only look on but even helped the pitiless Germans. After all, the Polish population was totally indifferent to the immense tragedy that overtook their Jewish fellow citizens, and in many cases even helped to exterminate the Jews.

Zaynvl's dream to have his children take over the forge after his own death was not realized. Two of his sons were already working with him, just as he had worked with his own father and eventually took over.

This was probably true of many of the hundreds of Jewish craftsmen in our town whose fate was similar.

Let these few words be a contribution to the small – but sacred – monument that this book constitutes. The book also commemorates all the other blacksmiths, shoemakers, tailors, carpenters, and other artisans, as well as merchants and all the other Jews who were exterminated so gruesomely by the German murderers, who were actively helped by many Poles as well as Ukrainians, Lithuanians, Latvians, and other blood-stained scoundrels.

Let the words also be a monument to the unknown grave of my devout parents and all my relatives who were tragically murdered.

* * *

Translator's footnotes:

1. Jewish tradition requires burials as soon as possible after death.
2. In 1821, Czar Nikolai instituted a conscription quota for Jewish males aged 12-25, requiring 25 years of army service. The children were placed in special "Cantonist Battalions" in training/educational establishments until the standard draft age of 18, when they began serving their 25 years.

[Page 114]

My Experiences During the Nazi Regime

by Yeshayahu Shtemer

September 29, 1939, was the beginning of our arduous journey. I went to Ludmir, then under Soviet authority. I could not find my place in Ludmir, and moved to Kostopil, a small town near Rivne. I discovered a few other Krasnystaw natives there: Shloyme and Yankev Kerpel, and Chayim-Meir Perlmuter.

On June 22, 1941, when war with the U.S.S.R. broke out, we decided to remain in Kostopil, hoping that we would eventually be able to go back home; we thought it would be the same home that we remembered.

As soon as the Germans entered Kostopil, we realized that things would go badly. We couldn't go home, and food grew ever more scarce. The attitude towards Jews immediately worsened. We had to steal a few potatoes in order to nourish ourselves and not starve to death. The potatoes kept us going for four weeks. Later, we were forced to work for the Germans, and received a bit of food in return.

On August 18, 1941, while at work, we heard that vehicles had come from Rivne, and people were being snatched up. No one knew what this meant.

We did not leave for a meal and tried to find out exactly what happened to the Jews who had been taken.

At 2 p.m., two German Gestapo officers came to our work site, accompanied by Ukrainian policemen. I did not like the looks

[Page 115]

of this and suggested to my friends that we escape. They hesitated – "we'll never make it" – and I left for the woods nearby, where I stayed until late that night. When I came back, none of my friends were there. I was told that 460 Jews had been taken that day, and no one knew what had happened to them.

We were sent to work again a few sad days later and were reassured that the remaining Jews would be safe and that we could go to work without worrying.

On Friday, September 18, 1941, I was sent with ten others to work for the police. We were assigned various jobs. No one had the slightest notion that we would never return, and we were being watched by a patrol. We finished working at 5 p.m. and wanted to leave but were ordered to continue working. We worked, tearfully, until nightfall, when we were sent down into a dark, damp cellar. When we asked for water, they told us

"You won't need water." As we sat in the dark cellar, we heard that graves were being prepared for us. We understood what awaited us, said our confession, and prepared to die, wishing only that it be quick.[1]

The night was endless. At dawn, we heard that more people from the town had come and were being stood in rows. This was the situation until 11 a.m. Every rustle and sound made us think that they were coming for us.

The cellar doors finally opened and we were ordered to go into the square. We stood in a row, and the commissioner asked who we were. A policeman responded that we were communists, but the translator said we were the men who had worked there the day before. The commissioner looked us up and down, and shouted, "I need young men to work in the cellar!" This happened as we were standing in rows and should have been marched to our deaths.

We were surrounded by watching Germans and policemen holding rubber whips, which they used to beat us mercilessly, not permitting us to cry. This continued until 2 p.m.

We returned to the cellar, which was not locked, and sat there for hours, not knowing what would happen to us, hearing shots

[Page 116]

constantly. The door suddenly opened, and a policeman appeared, who announced in Polish, "Sit calmly, you'll return home alive." We cued to sit and wait.

At nightfall, we were told that we could leave. They took all our possessions: boots, shoes, clothes, etc.

However, when we came home, there was no one there. The town was now Judenrein, purged of Jews. When I went out to the street the next morning, I saw only the chairman of the Judenrat, and a few people who had been freed with me.

A few days later, we were again taken and told that a camp would be established for the remaining Jews. I decided not to go, and left for Ludmir, walking only at night.

I found a different kind of existence in Ludmir. No one believed me when I told them about the events in Kostopil. The Jews were still living well and running their businesses. I started working in a mill, all the while thinking about returning to Krasnystaw. At one point I received a letter from my family that I'd be better off staying in Lublin, because all the Jews of Krasnystaw had been ordered to leave.

Six months passed. By this time a ghetto had been established in Ludmir as well, on April 18, 1942. Now a sense of impending doom hung over the community. Eight or ten people lived in a single room. Diseases began to spread, as did deaths.

The Commissioner now ordered the firing of all the Jews who worked in the mills (which were outside the ghetto). These Jews were in fact fired on June 1, 1942, and began to seek other jobs. My brother and I found employment in a barrel factory, where Chayim Buchbleter also worked. We all worked there until August 20, 1942. A new order came down: all the Jews who worked outside the ghetto now had to work inside it. There was very important government work to be done.

The work consisted of digging large pits one kilometer away from the town; they would be part of a tank position. They had to be 32 meters long, 21 meters wide, and 2.5 meters deep, and covered with earth on three sides.

[Page 117]

This project employed 3,000 Jews and continued until August 30, 1942. Some Jews really believed they were building tank positions, while others thought the pits would be graves for the few Jews still living in Ludmir.

There was talk of an operation targeting Jews. That turned out to be the case. At 5 a.m. on September 1, 1942, the ghetto was surrounded by Germans and policemen who began shooting into the ghetto from all sides. Anyone trying to escape was immediately shot on the spot. At 7 a.m., the murderers entered the ghetto and began catching Jews, beating and torturing them. Four friends and I had prepared a hideout, which we entered and stayed in for six days, without food. This operation lasted until September 15 and took a toll of 15,000 Jews. We sustained ourselves by eating vegetables from the gardens in the vicinity.

Jews reappeared after September 15 and reported that the commissioner had told them that all the remaining Jews would not be killed. About 1500 Jews came out of their hiding places. However, a few days later a new ghetto was designated for these survivors. A new Judenrat was formed, and Jews began to be sent to work again. More Jews arrived from the towns in the vicinity, and they now numbered about 3,000.

Another "operation" was held on November 13, 1942. We lay in a hideout again for six days and later ran to the forests.

The Gentiles of the villages around Ludmir reported that there were 400 Jews in that town again. We thus set out for Ludmir on May 8, 1943, but were not allowed into the ghetto. After much effort, my brother Mekhl and I were taken into the ghetto and were again sent to work in a barrel factory.

On December 13, 1943, another pogrom broke out, with the aim of exterminating the remainder of the Jews. We hid again, until December 18, when we went out in the city. Shots were fired at us as soon as we emerged. I fell to the ground, while my brother and the other six Jews escaped. I never saw my brother or the other Jews again. I returned to the hideout once again and stayed there for as long as my food held out; my food consisted of one cracker a day. I stayed there until January 2, 1944. When I had nothing left to eat, I had to go out. I walked

[Page 118]

aimlessly all night, sometimes encountering Germans, whom I was able to evade.

One night I went into a stable owned by a Gentile acquaintance and waited for daybreak. When the owner came in, I begged and wept to be allowed to hide in his house. He kept me in a room for two days and fed me. On the evening of the second day he took me to a hideout where eight more Jews were hiding. This continued until Liberation, on July 21, 1944. The Gentile, Leon Garczynski, is living in Poland.

Translator's footnote:

1. It is traditional for Jews to offer a final confession (Vidui) shortly before death.

[Unnumbered page]

Remember

May the Jewish nation remember its martyrs,
Including the martyrs of Krasnystaw who were killed, slaughtered,
Suffocated, and burned as part of
The Jewish nation during 1942-1943. Let the 22nd day
Of Iyar, the day of the mass murder
Of the Krasnystaw martyrs,
Be the day their names are mentioned
With those of all the Jewish martyrs
May God avenge their blood.

Remember what Amalek did to you![1]

Translator's footnote:

1. 22 Iyar 5702 is May 5, 1942. The Amalekites were a group that had fought bitterly with the Israelites who had left Egypt. Jews are commanded to "blot out their memory" (Deut. 25:19) in a phrase that is part of daily prayers.

[Pages 119-125]

List of the Jews Murdered in Krasnystaw
Transliterated by Vivian Singer

Edited by Yocheved Klausner

Family name(s)	First name(s)	Sex	Father's name	Mother's name	Name of spouse	Remarks	Page
א Alef							
EISEN	Chaim Shalom	M					119
EISEN		F			Chaim Shalom		119
EISENBERG	Dobe	F					119
EISENBERG		M		Dobe			119
EISENBERG		M		Dobe			119
OCHSENBERG	Aharon	M					119
OCHSENBERG		F			Aharon		119
EINWOHNER	Fischel	M					119
EINWOHNER		F			Fischel		119
EINWOHNER		F	Fischel				119
EIDELBERG	Hirsch	M					119
EIDELBERG		F			Hirsch		119
EIDELBERG		F	Hirsch				119
EIDELBERG	Heinich	M					119
EIDELBERG		F			Heinich		119
EISENSTEIN	Shimon Leib	M					119
EISENSTEIN		F					119
EISENSTEIN	Yoel	M					119
EISENSTEIN	Chaim Yaakov	M					119

Memorial Book of the Martyrs of Krasnystaw

EISENSTEIN		F			Chaim Yaakov		119
EINWOHNER	Tzirl	F					119
EINWOHNER		F		Tzirl			119
EICHENBLATT	Binyamin	M					119
OPAZDAWER	Chaim	M					119
OHN	Mechl	M				Son of the Shochet from Izbice	119
EINWOHNER	Israel	M					119
EIRELBERG	David	M					119
AWERUCH	Peretz	M					119
ACKERMAN	Avraham	M					119
EINWOHNER	Yaakov	M					119
EINWOHNER		F			Yaakov		119

ב Bet

BAUM	David	M					119
BLUMENKRANTZ	Fischel	M					119
BLUMENKRANTZ		F			Fischel		119
BAUM	Natan	M					119
BAUM		F			Natan		119
BERGERMAN		F					119
BERGERMAN	Simcha	M					119
BERGERMAN		F			Simcha		119
	Itche	M				Baker	119
BUCHBLAETTER	Mottel	M					119
BUCHBLAETTER		F			Motel		119
BINDER	Mendel	M					119
BLATT	Lipe	M					119
BLATT	Yaakov	M					119
BLATT	Rachel Lea	F					119
BIRNBAUM	Shaul Leib	M					119
BIRNBAUM		F			Shaul Leib		119
BELIK	Yechezkel	M					119
BELIK		F			Yechezkel		119
BORSTEIN	Leizer	M					119
BORSTEIN		F			Leizer		119
BORSTEIN	Beila	F					119
BUCHBLAETTER	Yehoshua	M					119
BRANDWEIN	Aharon	M					119
BELIK	Chava	F					119
BORSTEIN	David	M					120

Surname	First name	Sex					
BERGERMAN	Bluma	F					120
BAUMFELD	David	M					120
BLATT	Itche	M					120
BLATT	Moshe	M					120
BUCHEM	Simcha	M					120
BERMAN	Itche	M					120
BORSTEIN	Shmuel	M					120
BEITELMAN	Hersch	M					120
BERMAN	Pinchas	M					120
ג **Gimmel**							
GRINSTEIN	Tzirl	F					120
GERSTEIN	Berisch	M					120
GERSTEIN		F			Berisch		120
GOLDMAN	Moshe	M					120
GITT	Shlomo	M					120
GITT		F			Shlomo		120
GOLDBERG	Zeinwel	M					120
GOLDBERG	Gedalia	M					120
GERECHT		M				Shingle maker	120
GOLDMAN	Shlomo	M					120
GOLDMAN	Neta	M					120
GERTLER	Chaim	M					120
GERTLER	Aharon	M					120
GRASS	Meir	M					120
GARTLER	Sarah	F					120
		F		Sarah		Maiden name GARTLER	120
ד **Dalet**							
DEUTSCH	Itche	M					120
DREIER	Moshe	M					120
DREIER		F			Moshe		120
DRESCHER	Israel	M					120
DRESCHER		F			Israel		120
DRESCHER		F	Israel				120
DICK	Matel	M					120
DREIBLATT	Moshe	M					120
DREIBLATT		F			Moshe		120
DRECHSLER	Moshe	M					120
"DRAZSKAZS"	Neta	M					120
"DIGESS"	Dovid'l	M					120

Memorial Book of the Martyrs of Krasnystaw

ה Hey

HALBERSTAT	Shmuel	M			120
HARTSTEIN	Chana	F			120
HERTMAN	Melech	M			120
HERTMAN		F	Melech		120
HERTMAN	Hirsch	M			120
HARTMAN		F	Hirsch		120
HALPERN	Ben Zion	M			120
HALPERN		F	Ben Zion		120
HOCHMAN	Avraham	M			120
HARMAN	David	M			120
HOFFMAN	Betzalel	M			120
HOLZFIERER	Yidl	M			120
HERRING		M			120
HOLZHACKER	Israel	M			120
HOLZHACKER		F	Israel		120
HELFMAN	Getzel	M			120
HARTSTEIN	Menachem	M			120
HELFMAN	Heinich	M			120

ו Vav

WARSCHGITTER	Mendel	M			121
WEINSTEIN	Yosef	M			121
WALIK	Hersch	M			121
WEISS	Shlomo Yehoshua	M			121
WARSCHGITTER	Avraham Meir	M			121
WARSCHGITTER		F	Avraham Meir		121
WEISSWASSER	Noah	M			121
WEISSWASSER		M			121
WIESENBERG	Yehoshua	M			121
WALDMAN	Esther	F			121
VARMAN	Moshe	M			121
VARMAN		F	Moshe		121
VARMAN	Shmuel	M			121
VARMAN	Avisch	M			121
VARMAN	Nechemia	M			121
WEINRIEB	Lazer	M			121
WEINRIEB		F	Lazer		121
WANK	Wolf	M			121
WEISSERWASSER	Mordechai	M			121

WEISSERWASSER		F			Mordechai		121
VARMAN	Avraham	M					121
VARMAN		F			Avraham		121
WEINBERGER	Fischel	M					121
WEINBERGER		F			Fischel		121
WAGNER	Sarah	F					121

ז Zayin

SIEGELSCHIFFER	Moshe	M					121
SILBERMAN	Shmuel	M					121
SILBERMAN		F			Shmuel		121
SILBERMAN		F	Shmuel				121
SIEGELSCHIFFER	Mates [Matityahu]	M					121
SIEGELSCHIFFER		F			Mates [Matityahu]		121
SILBERZAHN	David	M					121
SILBERZAHN		F			David		121
SALTZMAN	Avraham	M					121
SALTZMAN		F			Avraham		121
SALTZMAN	Wolf Ber	M					121
SITZER	Yehoshua	M					121
SINGER	Moshe Leizer	M					121
SINGER		F			Moshe Leizer		121
	Hersch	M				Maker of soap	121
SALTZMAN	Chone	M					121
SALTZMAN		F					121
SINGER	Shalom	M					121
SEIFER	Yaakov	M					121
SEIFER		F			Yaakov		121
SILBERREICH	Mendel	M					121
SECHSER	Avraham	M					121
SILBERLICHT	Shlomo	M					121
SITZER		F			Herschel		121

ט Tet

TRAGER	Leibel	M					121
TRAGER	Yaakov	M					121
TRAGERMAN	Hirsch	M					121
TURAKELTAUB	Natan	M					121
TURAKELTAUB	Yaakov	M					121
TURAKELTAUB		F			Yaakov		121

Memorial Book of the Martyrs of Krasnystaw

TURGER	Zeinwel	M					121
TEITELBAUM	Israel	M					121

י Yod

"JASHLIKOVER"	Velvel	M					121
YOUNGMAN	Yaakov	M					121

כ Kaf

"CHRAMALINIK"	Yaakov	M					121
KATZ	Binyamin	M					121
KATZ	Avraham	M					121

ל Lamed

LERMAN	Moshe	M					122
LICHT	Berl	M					122
LEW	Israel Yaakov	M					122
LEW		F				Israel Yaakov	122
LANGMAN	Yaakov	M					122
LICHTZIEHER	Avraham	M					122
LEVKOWITZ	Shmuel Leizer	M					122
LEVKOWITZ		F				Shmuel Leizer	122
LERNER	Yaakov	M					122
LERNER		F				Yaakov	122
LERNER		F	Yaakov				122
LERNER	Yona	M					122
LERNER		F				Yona	122
LERNER	Simcha	M					122
LERNER		F				Simcha	122
LUFT	Baruch Hirsch	M					122
LUFT		F				Baruch Hirsch	122
LUFT		M	Baruch Hirsch				122
LOWENSTEIN	Israel	M					122
LOWENSTEIN		F				Israel	122
LUSTHAUS	Hirsch	M					122
LICHTSTEIN	Matel	M					122
LICHTSTEIN		F				Motel	122
LERMAN	Israel	M					122
LUSTHAUS	Moshe	M					122

Memorial Book of the Martyrs of Krasnystaw

LUSTHAUS	Efraim	M					122
LERMAN	Mechl	M					122
LUSTHAUS	Fischel	M					122
LANDER	Azriel	M					122

מ Mem

MUTTERPERL	Itche	M					122
MUTTERPERL		F			Itche		122
MUTTERPERL		M	Itche				122
MEHRENSTEIN	Avraham	M					122
MEHRENSTEIN		F			Avraham		122
MEHRENSTEIN	Hersch Baruch	M					122
MEHRENSTEIN		F				Mother of Hersh Baruch	122
MEHRENSTEIN		F				Sister of Hersh Baruch	122
MANDELTORT	Yona	M					122
MANDELTORT		F			Yona		122
MANDELTORT		M	Yona				122
MEIMAN	Gershon	M					122
MITTELMAN	Zeinwel	M					122
MANDLER	Itche	M					122
MANDLER		F			Itche		122
MARKEWITZ	Abba	M					122
MEHRENSTEIN	Shlomo	M					122
MEHRENSTEIN	Meir	M					122
MEHRENSTEIN	Yidel	M					122
"MOZSITZER"	Israel	M					122
MANDELTORT	Henia	F					122

נ Nun

NIRENBERG	Yehoshua	M					122
NIRENBERG		F			Yehoshua		122
NIRENBERG	Pinchas	M					122
NIRENBERG	Yidel	M					122
NIRENBERG	Hersch	M					122
NIRENBERG	Berl	M					122
NIRENBERG		F			Berl		122
NUSKER		M					122

ס Samech

STACK	Avraham	M					122

Memorial Book of the Martyrs of Krasnystaw

STACK		F		Avraham	122
ע Ayin					
ETTINGER	Velvel	M			122
ETTINGER	Moshe	M			122
ETTINGER	Tzadik	M			122
פ Peh					
PECHER	Avraham	M			122
FELDMAN		M			122
FIEGLER	Yehoshua	M			122
PERLMUTTER	Yaakov	M			122
PLETZL	Hersch	M			123
PECHTER	Israel	M			123
PECHTER		F		Israel	123
FLESCHLER	Shmuel	M			123
FLESCHLER	Chaia	F			123
PERLMUTTER	Shmuel	M			123
PERLMUTTER		F		Shmuel	123
PERLMUTTER	Baruch	M			123
PERLMUTTER	Mendel	M			123
PERLMUTTER		F		Mendel	123
PERLMUTTER		F	Mendel		123
PERLMUTTER	Baruch Yona	M			123
PINKER [FINKER]		M			123
PINKER [FINKER]		F		Matie	123
PINKER [FINKER]	Binyamin	M			123
PINKER [FINKER]		F		Binyamin	123
FEIGENBAUM	Hersch	M			123
FUTERMAN	Moshe	M			123
FUTERMAN		F		Moshe	123
FRIEDMAN	Yitzhak Aizik	M			123
FRIEDMAN		F		Yitzhak Aizik	123
FEIGENBAUM	Nute	M			123
FEIGENBAUM		F		Nute	123
FOIGELFUS [VOGELFUSS]	Leizer	M			123
FOIGELFUS [VOGELFUSS]		F		Leizer	123
FOIGELFUS [VOGELFUSS]		M	Leizer		123
FELDMAN	Levi	M			123

FELDMAN		F		Levi		123
FLUSSMAN	Avraham	M				123
FLUSSMAN		F		Avraham		123
FEUERSTEIN	Motel	M				123
FEUERSTEIN	Yosef	M				123
FINKEL	Efraim	M				123
PELTZ	Shlomo	M				123
PELTZ	David	M				123
PELZ		F		David		123
FERGER	Nute	M				123
PINKER [FINKER]	Leibel	M				123
PLOCK	Yidel	M				123
FELDMAN	Avigdor	M				123
FEIGENBAUM	Avigdor	M				123
FELDMAN	Moshe	M				123
FEIGENBAUM	Mates [Matityahu]	M				123
FISCHLER	Motel	M				123
FERDER	Yehoshua	M				123
FERDER		F			Mother of Yehoshua Ferder	123
PECHTER	Shaul	M				123
PECHTER		F	Yehoshua			123
PELZ	Rivka	F				123

צ Tzadek

ZUCKER		M				123
ZUCKERMAN	Avraham Baruch	M				123
ZUCKERMAN		M				123
ZUCKERMAN	Tzadok	M				123
ZUCKERMAN	Shmuel	M				123
ZUCKER	Yitzhak	M				123
ZUCKER	Yehoshua	M				123
ZUCKER	Avraham	M				123
ZUCKER		F		Avraham		123

ק Kuf

KOPPELMAN	Chava Roza	F				123
KNOBEL	Avraham	M				123
KUENSTLER	Rivka	F				123
KRAMER	Aharon	M				123
KROP	Shmuel	M				124

Memorial Book of the Martyrs of Krasnystaw

Surname	Given Name	Sex		Relation		Page
KROP	Itche	M				124
KUENSTLER	Yechiel	M				124
KUENSTLER	Moshe	M				124
KUPPERSTOCK	Leib	M				124
KANER	Israel	M				124
KANER		F		Israel		124
KASCHE	Avraham Yitzhak	M				124
KNABEL	Avisch	M				124
KNABEL		F		Avisch		124
KOLODNITZKI	Heinich	M				124
KNABEL	Israel	M				124
KASTELMAN	Anshel	M				124
KASTELMAN		F		Anshel		124
KASTELMAN		F	Anshel			124
KIRSCHENBAUM	Yaakov	M				124
KERPEL	Moshe	M				124
KERPEL	Motel	M				124
KORNFELD		F				124
KORNBRENNER	Mordechai	M				124
KORNBRENNER		F		Mordechai		124

ר Resh

Surname	Given Name	Sex		Relation		Page
ROSENBLUM	Yeshaia	M				124
ROSEN	Moshe	M				124
ROSENBLATT	Yitzhak	M				124
REICHSTEIN	Israel	M				124
ROSENSWEIG	Rafael	M				124
ROSENSWEIG		F		Rafael		124
REICHMAN	Lipe	M				124
ROSENBLATT	Yehuda	M				124
ROSENBLATT		F		Yehuda		124
ROITSTEIN	Avraham (Rabbi)	M				124
ROITSTEIN	Tzipe	F				124
"RIMER"	Hersch	M				124
"RIMER"		F		Hersch		124
REICHMAN	Yitzhak	M				124
ROBINSOHN	Leib	M				124
ROBINSOHN		F		Leib		124
REISS	Alter	M				124
REISS		F		Alter		124
REISS		F	Alter			124
ROSENBAUM	Issachar	M				124

REICHMAN	Mendel	M				124
ROSENBLATT	Zelig	M				124
ROSENBLATT	Avigdor	M				124
ROSENBAUM	Hersch	M				124

ש Shin

SCHACK	Perl	F				124
SCHNEIDER	Gedalia	M				124
STEIN	Avraham Mordechai	M				124
SCHWARZBIER	Chava	F				124
SPINDEL	Simcha	M				124
SPINDEL	Lazer	M				124
SCHACK	Mendel	M				124
SCHACK		F			Mendel	124
SCHACK	Yaakov	M				124
SCHACK		F			Yaakov	124
STONZEIGER	Tzvia	F				124
STONZEIGER	Nechemia	M				124
STONZEIGER	Yidel	M				124
SCHACK	Shimon	M				124
SCHACK		F			Shimon	124
SCHACK	Shaul	M				125
SCHACK		F			Shaul	125
SCHACK		F	Shaul			125
STEIN	Leibel	M				125
STEIN		F			Leibel	125
STEIN		F	Leibel			125
SCHNEIDWASSER	Avraham	M				125
STEMMER	Dische	F				125
STITZER	David	M				125
SCHACK	Heinich	M				125
SCHACK		F			Heinich	125
SCHACK	Moshe	M				125
SCHACK	Falik	M				125
SCHACK	Gershon	M				125
SCHNEIDER	Yosel	M				125
SCHNEIDWASSER	Meir	M				125
SMARAND	Melech	M				125
SMARAND		F			Melech	125

[Page 126]

Remnants

[Page 127]

[Blank]

[Page 128]

[Blank]

[Page 129]

The Survivors

When talking about survivors of Krasnystaw, the reference is usually to those who were living in the town when the war broke out in 1939. However, this terminology is not completely accurate.

Actually, with a few exceptions, the only survivors were those who left Krasnystaw before the German savages took control of the town, or immediately after their arrival. These people realized only at the last minute what their fate would be if they stayed in town; they fled to the Soviet Union, the only country where refuge was then still possible.

But there were many Krasnystaw residents who had gone to other countries years earlier. They had realized that they could not build a life in the town. They saw that the Jewish masses were gradually being pushed out of all the professions and could not make a living. The repressive Polish regime was forcing them to leave the town or be condemned to a life with no chance of advancement. They therefore decided to leave for other countries, where they believed there would be more freedom and other possibilities to realize their potential. I believe that those who left for America or other countries overseas years earlier had been much more prescient and willing to take risks than those who fled after the war broke out, right before the impending catastrophe. Obviously, those who

[Page 130]

had left to become Jewish settlers in the Land of Israel were really adventurous and revolutionary.

Thanks to their bravery, they and their children were saved from certain death and decline and should thus also be numbered among the survivors. Fate willed that those who had left Krasnystaw earlier would now become the main rescuers of those who survived destruction by the Nazis.

In fact, this is true not only of the Krasnystaw survivors but of all the Jewish survivors of the destruction. If it weren't for the Jews in America, most of whom are from Poland, the survivors would probably not be alive today. The material help from our brothers in the U.S.A. helped us, the survivors of the gas chambers and crematoriums, play a role in the resurrection of the Jewish people after the most recent destruction.

The Committee of Krasnystaw Natives in Germany

Seated (right to left): Noteh Abenshteyn, Yankev Shok, Aryeh Shtuntsayger, and Leybish Burshteyn
Standing: Mekhl Kanner, Avrom Varman, and Mordkhe Puterman

The enormous efforts being made to maintain and restore the lives of the few surviving Jews of Europe are closely linked with the dedication and goodwill of our American brothers. Help is reaching us through different channels: general national institutions as well as associations of natives.

This Yizkor Book, which is a monument to our murdered martyrs, must certainly also contain material about the survivors. May it be a consolation when we recount that our enemy could not destroy

[Page 131]

the entire Jewish nation, and that the survivors are continuing to spin the thread of Jewish history.

This is not the place to write about the general international efforts to support revival. We would only like to mention the unusual, extremely important work that the survivors' associations carried out to help their members with direct and timely material aid, as well as the organizational work of the survivors in the camps.

Our Krasnystaw natives in America do not lag behind the natives of other towns. Each person supports the general institutions, such as the "Joint," the Keren Kayemet, Keren Hayesod, and other national funds, and also donate directly to their fellow natives in the camps on the cursed, blood-soaked soil of Germany.[1]

Memorial Book of the Martyrs of Krasnystaw

Krasnystaw survivors at the first memorial service on May 5, 1947, in Bad Reichenhall, (Bavaria)

The main significance of this help lies not only in its material value, as important as it is. The few survivors, who felt so bereft after the destruction, needed, above all,

[Page 132]

the encouragement and cheer supplied by a warm word, to enable them to continue their lives. Above all, they needed a warm brotherly hand to demonstrate that they had not been forgotten and left lonely and neglected.

The main reason the survivors decided to organize in associations was their desire to meet once again with familiar people from their hometown. People wanted to huddle close to each other; they all felt orphaned. For this reason, as well as the desire to mourn those martyred – brothers, sisters, fathers, mothers, and friends – in community, our Krasnystaw survivors' association was formed.

Fate had decreed that in 1939, when the Nazi flood overwhelmed Poland and drew near to our town, a certain number of people had the opportunity to save themselves in the Soviet Union. About one hundred people then fled at that time and are today the only survivors of the Krasnystaw Jewish community. Those who stayed in the town and were overtaken by the Nazi occupation were gruesomely murdered and annihilated. Miraculously, three young women also survived: Esther Muterperl (daughter of Itshele Muterperl); Esther Knobel (daughter of Abish Knobel, and Tzipora

Krasnystaw survivors at the second solemn memorial day for the martyrs of Krasnystaw, May 12, 1948, in Bad Reichenhall (Bavaria)

[Page 133]

Zigelshifer (the daughter of Yitzchok Zigelshifer) who was tortured so severely and was so weak that she died in Germany. A few young people also survived, due to the fact that they were shipped to Germany for hard labor and lived there under Aryan names. All the others were taken, together with the Jews from the surrounding towns, to Belzec, where they were murdered. Many of them were murdered in Krasnystaw proper.

Only those who had fled to the Soviet Union and had lived there for five years under various conditions finally returned to Poland. The few dozen Krasnystaw natives who returned from the U.S.S.R. after the war were like twigs broken off an enormous tree.

It was mostly the young who went to the U.S.S.R. Older people did not go. No one could have imagined that the Germans would murder everyone in the devilishly refined manner that they did – old, young, men, women, and children. The older people thought, "Jews are accustomed to having problems, and people prefer to die in their own beds." They couldn't imagine that the murderers wouldn't allow people to die in their own beds, and that the dead wouldn't even be buried in a Jewish cemetery.

Those in the Soviet Union had no idea of the scope of the disaster. People heard what Hitler had been doing to the Jews, and their hearts contracted with worry for the fate of their nearest and dearest: mothers, fathers, and families. But these thoughts were shoved aside: "Such cruelty is impossible," "the world won't be silent." In each of us there lived a spark of hope that we would make it through the dark days and meet our nearest and dearest once again.

That was also why all the Polish Jews hurried back once the war was over. But they did not find their dear ones, only emptiness and desolation. The Krasnystaw survivors went back to their town fearing for their lives, as rampaging gangs of ruffians were freely attacking Jews there.

The Jewish homes were now occupied by non-Jews, and there was no trace of family members. The survivors fled as though from an epidemic, chased by the dark, bloody nightmare of destruction, and wandered all over Poland. It was then that they decided to leave Poland with no clear destination, and ended up in the displaced-persons camps.

Thanks to two enterprising people, a meeting of Krasnystaw survivors was held in Bad Reichenhall on May 5, 1947. Many tears

[Page 134]

were shed that day. People swore to remember the martyrs forever.

People sought consolation among our fellow natives in America and elsewhere. It was not material help – although that was also needed – as much as warm words of sharing in grief. I would like to emphasize that the first words of sympathy came from the Committee in Los Angeles. The first letter from the chairman, our dear Ben Tsukerman, was worth more than the greatest treasure. The Los Angeles Committee also sent material help, through Ben Tsukerman. Although Los Angeles was the home of only a few of our hometown survivors, they sent more help than any of the other committees combined. Hundreds of food packages and dozens of packages with clothes arrived, thanks to Ben alone.

Ben Tsukerman also sent money to each survivor. I would like to emphasize the manner in which this help was extended: always wholeheartedly, and with care for the recipients' humanity.

Krasnystaw survivors at the first solemn commemoration, May 5, 1959, in Bad Reichenhall, Bavaria

[Page 135]

Ben Tsukerman, the distinguished chairman of the Los Angeles Committee was the chief force behind the creation of this memorial book.

The main achievements of the Los Angeles Committee are, without question, preservation of the memory of the murdered Jews of Krasnystaw as well as the help extended to the survivors.

The work of the Krasnystaw survivors' organization in Germany would certainly not have been possible without the help of Ben Tsukerman and the Los Angeles Committee.

Our fellow survivors in New York as well, headed by President Sam Lichtenshteyn, did not forget their sacred duty towards their unhappy brothers in the DP camps. The New York Aid Committee is continuing its assistance by sending money to many individual survivors.

We heard that an Aid Committee was formed in Argentina as well, headed by Mr. Gershn Shtern. Unfortunately, we have as yet not been able to be in close contact with the Argentina Aid Committee due to distance and communication issues. However, we are convinced that all the Krasnystaw survivors, wherever they are, are committed to carrying out the last will and testament of the martyrs: making sure that the memory of Jewish Krasnystaw shall not disappear, and that the Jewish people shall continue to exist.

May the participants be blessed!

Translator's footnote:

1. The "Joint" is the American Jewish Joint Distribution Committee, a Jewish relief organization based established in 1914 and based in New York City. Keren Kayemet LeYisrael (Jewish National Fund) is a non-profit organization founded in 1901 to buy land and encourage Jewish resettlement in Israel. Keren Hayesod (literally "The Foundation Fund") is an official fundraising organization for Israel with branches in 45 countries. Keren Hayesod works in coordination with the Government of Israel and the Jewish Agency for Israel to further the national priorities of the State of Israel.

[Page 136]

My Last Visit to Krasnystaw

By Aryeh Shtuntsayger

In November of 1944, I was sent from the USSR to Lublin as a soldier in the Polish army. Naturally, my first thought was to take advantage of the chance to travel to Krasnystaw. I had already heard in the USSR of the disaster that had overtaken our people and the destruction of Polish Jewry. But the reports were so gruesome and unbelievable that everyone felt they had to see it with their own eyes. I had a lingering spark of hope: "Maybe it was exaggerated, maybe the decimation wasn't that total."

When I arrived in Lublin, the first thing I had to do was to report to Headquarters. The commander told me at the train station that Headquarters was located in the notorious Majdanek death camp. Curiosity drove me there as soon as possible. I wanted to see the death camp where millions of our brothers, sisters, fathers and mothers were murdered.

The camp was about four kilometers from the city, covered an area of 14 square kilometers, and was surrounded by a double barbed-wire fence. Dozens of barracks stood in straight rows. This was where the unfortunates condemned to death were kept while alive. The camp was in perfect order. Paved roads separated the barracks. There was no sign of the terrible tragedy that played out here, between these fences. Almost all the barracks were now populated by soldiers. I

[Page 137]

looked around intently, hoping to find a trace of those who were murdered. On the right, I noticed a partly ruined building with a protruding chimney.

The soldiers told me that it was the crematorium. I went up to the half-destroyed structure: the oven was almost intact. Inside, there were huge iron grates with perforations. I was told that these were meant to allow the fat to flow off the burning bodies into a channel; the fat was later used to make soap.

Mounds of human bones and ash lay around the crematorium. Shoes of all sizes, including women's and children's shoes, were strewn around the warehouses.

The moment I had a chance the next morning, I went to the city, with the sole aim of finding an acquaintance, or just any Jew. I was very familiar with Lublin before the war. There were many people I knew there, as well as family members. I went to Lubartowska Street, where my uncle had had a sausage factory. Naturally, not only could I not find the factory or my uncle; I could not see any sign of Jews throughout the full length of the street, which had been populated by Jews. All the Jewish shops now bore Polish names. My heart contracted when I saw the street calmly going about its business. The Jews had all vanished, yet everything seemed so normal...

I asked a Christian whether there were any Jews anywhere. He told me that there were Jews in the Peretz-House.[1] I went there, and found about 200 Jewish men and women who had survived the concentration camps. Most of them were Polish Jews; there were also some Jews from Hungary. All were from locations far from Lublin, and none from the Lublin area.

I told those Jews that I was planning to go to Krasnystaw. They advised me not to go, because at that time Krasnystaw was the center of the A.K. and the N.S.Z.[2] No Jew's life was safe there.

Downcast, I returned to Headquarters. I was then posted to the Fifth Special Battalion, and sent to the front at Dêblin, near the Vistula River. But I clung to the notion of visiting Krasnystaw. A few months later, as soon as I could get a furlough, I went there. For added security, I took my adjutant along. He was a Pole who looked Jewish and was strangely friendly. His Jewish appearance may have contributed to his affinity for Jews.

[Page 138]

Armed with a Parabellum and a TT, as well as several hand grenades in my pocket, I drove to Krasnystaw.[3] My adjutant carried an automatic.

The moment I got out of the car in Krasnystaw, I felt terribly lonely. Where should I go? I had a look at the town. It had hardly been damaged in the fighting; the buildings were whole. But on that cold, gray winter day the town looked sad and neglected. The buildings around us, mostly Jewish property, were dilapidated and filthy. Apparently, the facades hadn't been repaired since the Jews were driven out of town. The main square that had been so beautiful was now derelict, and the fence around it was broken.

I decided to visit my home first. But as I went into the courtyard, my heart sank. Here, where Jewish children had played, all was deathly silent. The windows used to be hung with curtains decorated with crystals. I walked around the courtyard for a few minutes. No one came out. It was desolate.

My mind filled with thoughts, and my heart beat strongly. Here, in this corner, my father and I built a sukkah every year. Over there is where I used to sit and read on summer evenings or play the mandolin. And this is where my little sister fell and was badly bruised while playing.

I left the courtyard, practically at a run, and did not go into our apartment. I knew that I'd never go there again. But I decided to take a good look at the town; I knew every corner of it very well.

It happened to be a market day, and I went to the marketplace. No Jews were around. Christians dealt with the very same merchandise that Jews used to handle. I walked between the stalls. One Christian was selling used goods, which he had probably "inherited" from Jews. Others came by to inspect the merchandise. He demanded a high price. When the peasant women began to negotiate with him, he shouted, "After all, I'm not a Jew who sets a high price!"

I felt another stab in my heart and was tempted to throw a grenade at the Christian and his merchandise. But I restrained myself and kept walking. No one realizes I'm Jewish, I suddenly thought.

The old hazelnut tree still stood in the middle of the marketplace, as it did when I would climb it as a child to pick the nuts. Later, I went to the town's

[Page 139]

House of Study. The structure was a ruin, and the windows were boarded up. It now served as storage for the local Cooperative. I was heartsick when I remembered that here, in the House of Study, I had been a student for several years. We students owned the street. Now it was empty and sad, and the boarded-up windows were scary in their blindness and destruction.

I continued to the "club," where I had spent the best days of my life. It was a center for discussions and readings, where nearly all the young people of Krasnystaw went to relax and hang out. The club was my school for social matters, where I took my first steps as an organizer and social activist, and developed my outlook on life. The club and the House of Study planted a profound, ongoing reverence forouse of Study, House of books in me and in many other young people of Krasnystaw. This was where I went to an evening dance for the first time and was first excited by girls. The library was destroyed in the first days of the war, as soon as the Hitlerist vandals entered the town. A Christian was now living there. It was the same in the Turiisk Hassidic small synagogue. The square, where almost every Jew in the town had played as a child, was now bare. The nearby schoolrooms for small boys was where Reb Leyzer the melamed taught for forty consecutive years. Images of my earliest childhood danced before my eyes.

I went to the bridge, the location of my first date, my first evening walk with a girl, and my first bashful kiss… The road to the bridge, which also led to the train station, was paved with gravestones robbed from the defiled Jewish cemetery. As soon as I noticed this, I felt as though I was walking over live coals. I turned to the right and walked through the Groblie neighborhood, which had been populated almost exclusively by poor Jews. Scenes of Shabbat afternoons filled my vision: the hard-working, perennially worried Jewish women would sit down for a rest on thresholds and the earthen benches adjoining the walls and share good-natured gossip about each couple that passed by. I passed the small bridge near the Groblie House of Study. There was no trace of the House of Study now; it had become a vegetable garden. The Jews of Groblie would cross the bridge every Shabbat afternoon and go to the hill, to drink their fill of the crystal-clear, ice-cold water of the spring. Not one of these hardworking Jewish laborers remains; they have all vanished. I felt ants crawling over my back, and shuddered.[4] My brain seemed unresponsive, as though weighed down by a layer of lead. But I had decided to see everything, and continued walking.

[Page 140]

The smithy, where Zaynvl the blacksmith and his brother had worked, was still there, but the building was now locked.

There was only one more site that I had to see: the Jewish cemetery. I walked to it.

It was outside the town, on the border of a pine forest. This was where my grandparents rested, and where pious Jews shed their tears during troubled times, begging the deceased to intercede for them "there," with God, for the sake of their children.

The cemetery had been defiled in a terrible way. The fence was destroyed, shards of gravestones littered the ground, and the graves were trampled and buried. I could not look at the appalling sight; my eyes filled with heavy tears that rolled down my face. The few peasants who walked by stopped to watch the Polish soldier who was standing there weeping. They soon realized what was happening and went on their ways. I was seized by the strange feeling that I needed to leave as quickly as possible. "The Christians must not see my tears," I thought.

Night had fallen in the meantime. I went to the train station, hoping to find a train to Lublin. I wanted to flee from the town as soon as possible; my town had suddenly become a completely alien place, and I felt terribly lonely and crushed. But there was no train. I had to wait until morning and started thinking about a place to spend the night.

I met a young peasant at the train station, a blacksmith named Halas, with whom I had gone to school. He didn't recognize me, and thought I was Polish. He came up to us, expressed his esteem for the "Polish officer," and invited us to stay with him. I went to his rundown hut.

That evening, my adjutant played his mandolin, and a couple of young Christians came by to talk with the "Polish officer." They told me they belonged to the AK; I decided to be careful. To make sure they wouldn't suspect me of being Jewish, I had to clear my face of all agitation and sadness. I explained that I came from this region and was passing through. I asked them what had happened here during the years of occupation. They calmly told me about the extermination of the Jews, as though it was a natural, ordinary thing. The host boasted that he had not benefited from Jewish property, and was as poor as he had been before, unlike other people. Because of this, I was not completely sure that I was unrecognized; the Jewish face of my Christian

[Page 141]

adjutant was suspect. I spent the night wide-awake, revolver in hand.

I went into town very early to locate a car, but had to wait for several hours. As I walked, I was recognized by a few Christians. One of them, a former bricklayer, came up. I immediately noticed that he had a problem speaking to me. He was awkward and uncomfortable. I wanted to try and recognize his voice, and asked him, "Do you think I should come back here and settle?" "Yes, you could do that," he said, "there's space. But…" he stopped, then continued, "There are some horrible people here, and that makes it terrible."

I sensed that he was telling the truth. Jews did not bother him, poor bricklayer that he was. But the others, who had enriched themselves by grabbing Jewish houses and Jewish businesses, would not permit a Jew to live here, knowing as he does how they obtained their wealth.

I had no thought of paying another visit, because my heart wouldn't survive in this atmosphere; it would break.

The car arrived. I got in quickly, so as to leave the place as soon as possible.

When the car began moving, a terrible curse burst out of my chest, a curse with no addressee. It would lurk here, and locate those who helped in the destruction.

But this nebulous curse depressed me even more.

Translator's footnotes:

1. The Peretz House in Lublin, named after the great Jewish writer and cultural figure Yitzchok Leybush Peretz (1852-1915), was built as the seat of a school, a library and cultural institutions. After the war it functioned as a center of Jewish life in the city and served as a shelter for people who had lost their belongings during the war.
2. A.K. were the initials of the Armia Krajowa (Polish Home Army); N.S.Z. were the initials of the Narodowe Siły Zbrojne (National Armed Forces). Both organizations were anti-Semitic.
3. The Parabellum was a German semi-automatic pistol; the TT was a Soviet semi-automatic pistol.
4. This expression is the equivalent of "chills running up my spine".

[Page 142]

Redress for Jewish Souls

By Noyekh Griss

When my father visited the Land of Israel before World War I, he promised several people from our town to bring them the precious gift they asked for: a small bag of soil from the Holy Land. It was the gift they most wished for. They believed that they could only complete their lives through uniting with the soil of the Holy Land, and it would fulfill their deepest desires.

The deep and widespread faith, expressed in innumerable legends, that Jews needed to become one with their soil after death, if not in life, guided most Jews and was expressed in various ways. It was this faith that gave rise to all the forms of Zionism.

Whereas Jews had once brought soil for pious men and women, a delegation from the Land of Israel had now brought its soil to the grave of the Warsaw Ghetto heroes, emphasizing the continuity between their battle and ours as links in the chain that calls for our freedom to be Jews and to live as Jews.

Thanks to the current auspicious democratic conditions, it has become possible to erect a monument to the fighters of the Warsaw Ghetto. However, there are dozens and hundreds of cities, towns, fields, and forests throughout Poland, France, Hungary, Germany, Romania, and Belgium, where it may not be possible to erect monuments. There are graves that will remain unknown, and there are people who do not know where their relatives' graves lie.

That is not all. We need to not only honor the memory of the deceased, though millions were murdered and no trace of their remains exists.

[Page 143]

The survivors have another duty: to immortalize an entire generation in a way that will express their immense bravery when they died to sanctify the nation.

It was no coincidence that, on the 42d day of the heroic fight in the Warsaw Ghetto, when the ghetto was in flames, Jews barricaded themselves inside the last four-story building still standing

"When the flames enveloped the first floor, the Jews climbed to the second floor, and then continued to climb, fleeing the inexorable fire, up to the fourth floor. The enemies yelled in vain, 'Come down! We'll grant you your lives!' The last defenders of Jewish honor did not wish to live as slaves; the battle continued.

"Suddenly, the savage German soldiers stood as though turned into stone, with their weapons in numb hands. The scene on the eerie unearthly street was strange: the last four defenders, remnants of the heroic fighters, came out onto the highest balcony. Each was wrapped in a flag – one in red, another red and white, a third blue and white. The fourth was not a flag at all, but rather a tallit.[1] Enveloped in their flags, they sounded a heartrending, unearthly cry: 'Am Yisro'el Chai!'[2] Then they flung themselves into the fire" (Yudel Mark, *Ruins Recount*).[3]

Am Yisro'el Chai was the battle cry. Where else but here would the dream of Jewish fighters come true? Where else but here should their heroism be commemorated?

The names and actions of Anielewicz and Hannah Szenes, as well as Braslav and Frumkeh should be engraved in the future "Hall of Heroism."[4] Others whose voices should be heard are Meir Hazanovitch, Trumpeldor, Brenner, Yoysef Lewartowski, Leyb Yaffe, and Dr. Kahane of Kielce.[5] The same is true for the millions of European Jews and the hundreds of Jews in the Land of Israel who recently fell so that our people might live.

There is no doubt that the Jews who fought in the battle against Fascism will be properly honored in each country separately.

The new Poland serves as an example. The underground fighters (Maquis) in France received medals. When Spain is free again, the Jewish fighters of the Botwin Company will be among those honored.[6] But there must be a site and an institution that will collect the Jewish contributions, and build the monumental structure of Jewish heroism. People have been thinking about specific monuments in all cities and countries, and various institutions have been created for this purpose. However, I remember the great impression made on the Polish Historical Commission

[Page 144]

by our delegate's information from the London Conference on Yad Vashem in 1945.

He told us about the gigantic project that would build a mausoleum in Jerusalem, a Temple of Heroism that would function as a historical research institute and would include a library, an archive, etc.

We gradually began to think of ourselves as a branch of the Central Jewish Institute. Almost all the researchers thought that their work would take place in Jerusalem. It was similar in Prague. I visited the Museum and was interested in materials from Terezin. I was told that the materials were already in the Land of Israel.

The Historical Commission in Germany is also collecting material and does not plan to stay in that accursed land.

The center for documentation in Paris is also strongly connected with Yad Vashem, as are many other institutions.

The Yad Vashem idea is outstanding in its simplicity and obviousness. It will redress the souls of the millions who were buried without a grain of soil from the Land of Israel; those who are unburied, and whose ashes nourish the fields of Europe.

Yad Vashem has several other important missions. It must be an institution that perpetuates the idea of passing knowledge on to younger generations and makes sure that national memory persists.

There are people who would like to forget everything that happened, and do not think that the tragedy could return. People are leading their lives as though nothing had happened. This is terrible. A people with a short memory, that does not wish to learn from the past, and forgets its dead, is destined to disappear. This cannot be allowed to happen. Yad Vashem must therefore be a flexible, wide-ranging institution. It must combine the static elements of emotional memory so important for the Jews with a powerful dynamism of national historical significance for the people.

The nation must understand this and help, so that all the elements of this grand plan will be transformed into plans and actions.

Translator's footnotes:

1. A tallit is a fringed garment worn as a prayer shawl by religious Jews. These often were white with blue stripes.
2. "The nation of Israel lives" -- a traditional declaration affirming Jewish existence.
3. Yehuda (Yudl) Mark (1897-1975) was a prolific scholar, educator, and writer. The book mentioned was published in 1947.

4. Mordecai Anielewicz (1919-1942) led the Jewish Fighting Organization in the Warsaw Ghetto. Hannah Szenes (1921-1944) was parachuted into Europe by the British army to aid in the war effort. Shmuel Braslav (1920-1942) was a key figure in the Jewish Fighting Organization in the Warsaw ghetto. Frumkeh (Fruma Plotnicka, 1914 – 1943) was a fighter in the Warsaw Ghetto and other ghettos of Europe. The "Hall of Heroism" seems to have been an idea (never realized) to commemorate the events in Warsaw.
5. Meir Hazanovitch (1890-1913) was a Zionist activist who was killed as a watchman in Palestine. Joseph Trumpeldor (1880-1920) was a Zionist activist and Russian army hero, who was killed defending a Jewish settlement in Palestine. Yosef Haim Brenner (1881-1921) was a Hebrew-language author from the Russian Empire, and one of the pioneers of modern Hebrew literature, who was killed by Arabs near Tel Aviv. Yoysef Lewartowski (1896-1943) was a Zionist activist in the Warsaw Ghetto who was murdered in Treblinka. Leyb Yaffe (1878-1948) was a Zionist leader and cultural figure, who was killed in an explosion in Jerusalem. Dr. Sewerin Kahane was the head of the local Jewish Committee in Kielce, Poland, and was killed during the pogrom of July 1946.
6. This was a Jewish unit of the International Brigades in 1937, during the Spanish Civil War.

Memorial Book of the Martyrs of Krasnystaw

[Page 145]

List of Surviving Krasnystaw Jews

Ayzen, Simcha
Aynvoner, Chayim and Rivka
Aynvoner, Betzalel
Eydelsberg, Eliya
Eydlsberg, Nochem
Eydlsberg, Moyshe and Nekheh
Avrukh, Sheyndl
Avrukh, Shmuel and Chayeh
Avrukh, Soreh
Avrukh, Tsirl
Obenshteyn, Noteh and wife
Obenshteyn, Yoysef
Obenshteyn, Goldeh
Ayznshteyn, Perl
Oksenberg, Pinkhes and Rokhl
Ayznshteyn, Perl
Bergerman, Yitzchok
Bergerman, Yitzchok[1]
Bergerman, Akiva
Burshteyn, Leybish and Sima
Burshteyn, Toybeh
Burshteyn, Soreh
Bukhshteyn, Shmuel
Bukhshteyn, Dovid
Bekher, Noyekh
Batalion, Dovid

Gut, Shimshon
Grinshteyn, Sheyndl
Gershteyn, Avrom
Dreyer, Yoysef
Dreyer, Royzeh
Dreyer, Mirl

Dresher, Meir
Holtshacker, Dovid
Hartshteyn, Borekh
Hokhboym, Azriel
Hokhboym, Azriel[1]
Valik, Rokhl
Vaynrib, Moysheh
Vaynrib, Matess
Varman, Avrom and Esther
Zilberman, Tsvi
Zaltsman, Hersh and Sheyndl
Zaltsman, Dovid
Zaltsman, Leybl
Zitser, Hersh
Zinger, Tsudik
Zaltsman, Pesyeh
Zaltsman, Shmuel
Zaltsman, Mendl
Zaltsman, Tsirl
Zaltsman, Hindeh

Bukhbleter, Berl	Zaltsman, Leya
Boym, Feygeh	Zaltsman, Miryam
Belik, Hersh and brother	Turkltoyb, Nochem
Birnboym, Dvoyre	Turkltoyb, Leybl
Gerekht, Moysheh	Lev, Rokhl
Grobshtok, Hersh	Luft, Goldeh
Grobshtok, Motl	Luft, Rivka
Grobshtok, Tsirl	Lander, Shimen
Grobshtok, Feyge	Lander, Meir
Gartler, Nochem	Lerner, Khone
Goldberg, Yoysef	Lerner, Aaron

[Page 146]

Muterperl, Esther	Raykhman, Miryam
Mandltort, Faleh	Rozntsvayg, Mendl and wife
Mandltort, Yisro'el	Shok, Dovid
Mandltort, Hersh-Leyb	Shok, Aaron-Yitschok
Mandler, M. F.	Shok, Uri
Nirenberg, Yidl	Shok, Uri and Chayeh
Stok, Motl	Shok, Yankev and Tsipora
Fingerhut, Soreh	Shok, Rokhl
Fingerhut, Mordkhe	Shok, Mendl
Prekhter, Borekh and Esther	Shok, Mekhl
Prekhter, Moyshe and Esther	Shok, Libeh
Prekhter, Eliya	Shok, Moyshe
Prekhter, Beyleh	Shok, Osher and Etkeh
Prekhter, Miryam	Shok, Leybl and Soreh
Peltz, Tsudik	Shok, Yitzchok and wife
Perlmuter, Yoysef	Shok, Moysheh
Fleshler, Reuven	Shok, Simcheh
Flusman, Yekutiel	Shtuntsayger, Mordkheh

Memorial Book of the Martyrs of Krasnystaw

Futerman, Avrom	Shtuntsayger, Moysheh and Yocheved
Futerman, Mordkhe and Hindeh	Shyuntsayger, Aryeh
Feldman, Berish	Shtuntsyger, Brayndl
Finkel, Perl	Shtuntsayger, Soreh
Kenobl, Esther	Shtuntsayger, Gitl
Kanner, Mekhl	Shtuntsayger, Dovid
Kanner, Leyzer	Shtuntsayger, Yisro'el
Kestlman, Yankev	Shtuntsayger, Yitskhok
Kornbrener, Yekutiel	Shtuntsayger, Binyomin
Rozenblat, Yankev and Rivka	Shtemer, Yeshaya
Raykhman, Leyzer	Shvarts, Khaneh

Translator's footnote:

1. Some names appear more than once in the original document.

[Page 147]

Notes of Thanks

We express our heartfelt thanks to all those who have helped this project thus far and continue their active work and support for their surviving brothers and sisters of Krasnystaw, enabling the publication of this book, the only monument to our murdered martyrs.

Below we present their names. We send them our good wishes and wish them much luck. May their sacred, noble work be crowned with success.

Aryeh Shtuntsayger
* * *

The Krasnystaw Association in New York extends whole-hearted thanks to all the members who actively supported and contributed to help our brothers and sisters in the camps, and sends regards to the following members in New York.[1]

Sam and Helen Lichtenstein and family
President of the Krasnystaw Association of New York

Gedalia and Sima Kats and family
Avrom Lichtenstein and family
Mr. and Mrs. E. Kesselman, Treasurers
Mr. and Mrs. Y, Finkelstein, Finance Secretaries
Mr. and Mrs. Lebensbaum, Committee
Mr. and Mrs. S. Weiss, Committee
Mr. and Mrs. Luftik, Committee
Mr. and Mrs. Edler, Committee
Mr. and Mrs. Kutshman
Mr. and Mrs. Max Hertz
Mr. and Mrs. Wegener,
Mr. Milton and Mrs. Charlotte Lichtstein

[Page 148]

The Yankev Statman Memorial Fund Los Angeles

The Yankev Statman Memorial Fund in Los Angeles extends its heartfelt thanks to all its members and all those who actively and materially supported the Fund's sacred work to help all Krasnystaw natives everywhere, and to safeguard the memory of our martyrs, by erecting a monument and by publishing this Yizkor Book. We send our best regards to the following persons.

Memorial Book of the Martyrs of Krasnystaw

Los Angeles

Yankev Statman (may he rest in peace)
Rivka Statman and
Irving Statman
Max and Becky Bergman
Moyshe and Andree Goldberg
Shloyme and Celia Tsukerman
Tsaduk Tsukerman
Yoysef and Rokhl Simon

Frank and Jenny Simon
Fayvel Boymfeld
Yoysef and Regina Zayd
Sam and Masha Vership
Chayim and Fanny Haken
Mr. and Mrs. David Gordon
Philip and Shirley Roznblum

Canada

Berl and Malka Maymon
Yoysef Maymon

Mr. and Mrs. Leyzer Gold
Leyzer and Khane Grinberg

Chicago

Leybl and Frida Lerman
Netanel and Mrs. Maymon
Mendl Kahn

Max Kahn
Geni Kahn

[Page 149]

Detroit

Tsukerman Family Members:
Ben and Minnie Tsukerman

(President of the Yankev Statman Memorial Fund)

Binyomin and Rosie Tsukerman

Aaron Yoysef and Yocheved Hershteyn
Louis and Annie Zak

Louis and Rose Grand

Memorial Book of the Martyrs of Krasnystaw

Max and Polly Tsukerman
Harry and Nettie Tsukerman
Yankev and Ida Tsukerman
Yitzchok and Rosie Tsukerman

Mr. Velvl Zak
Yisro'el and Mashl Tsukerman
Esther Miller

We send you our best wishes and wish you happiness

New York

Alter and Mildred Hokhman
Esther Muterperl
Mr. and Mrs. Henry Bergman
Mr. and Mrs. Shloyme Leybish
and Chayeh Ayzenberg
Doris Ayzenberg
Mr. and Mrs. Max Hertz
Mr. and Mrs. Hersh Fayvl Kuni
Mr. and Mrs. Berger
Mr. and Mrs. Sam Epstein
Yitschok Tsukerman
Mr. and Mrs. Fayvl Hershteyn
Prof. Jacob Yaffe and Esther
Gitl Yaffe
Yankev and Yitskhok Dresher
and families
Mr. and Mrs. Chayim Hershteyn
Sam Schwarts and family
Louis and Mrs. Silverberg and
family

[Page 150]

The Committee of Krasnystaw Survivors Exiled in Germany

We heartily thank our townspeople overseas, who extended a helping hand to their surviving brothers in the camps.

Special thanks to the Chairman of the Krasnystaw Organization in Los Angeles, Mr. Ben Tsukerman, for his remarkably warm attitude and understanding of the needs of Krasnystaw survivors and for his initiative in publishing this Memorial Book.

Yankev Shok, Chairman	Hersh Zaltsman
Aryeh Shtuntsayger, Secretary	Leyzer Kornfeld
Mordkhe Futerman, Treasurer	Meir Dresher
Avrom Varman	

Translator's footnote:

1. The camps referred to are the Displaced Persons (DP) camps created in Europe following World War II.

NAME INDEX

A

Abenshteyn, 141
Abramovich, 22
Abramovitsh, 88
Ackerman, 129
Anielewicz, 156, 158
Avrukh, 159
Aweruch, 129
Aydelberg, 114
Aykhenboym, 86
Aynvoner, 159
Ayzen, 159
Ayzenberg, 16, 20, 24, 105, 164
Ayznshteyn, 159

B

Baldan, 62
Batalion, 159
Baum, 129
Baumfeld, 130
Beilis, 96
Beitelman, 130
Bekher, 159
Belik, 129, 160
Berger, 164
Bergerman, 24, 129, 130, 159
Bergman, 163, 164
Berman, 119, 130
Binder, 24, 106, 115, 116, 129
Binyomeles, 118
Birnbaum, 129
Birnboym, 109, 160

Blat, 19, 20, 24
Blatt, 129, 130
Blum, 86
Blumenkrantz, 129
Blumshteyn, 118
Borstein, 129, 130
Boym, 24, 160
Boymfeld, 24, 25, 54, 115, 163
Brandwein, 129
Braslav, 156, 158
Brenner, 156, 158
Broniewski, 68, 70
Buchbinder, 24
Buchblaetter, 129
Buchbleter, 124
Buchem, 130
Bukhbleter, 160
Bukhshteyn, 159
Burshteyn, 141, 159
Burshtin, 112

C

Chramalinik, 133
Czar Nikolai, 121

D

De Hirsch, 64
Deutsch, 130
Dick, 130
Digess, 130
Drayblat, 20, 24
Drazskazs, 130

Drechsler, 130
Dreiblatt, 130
Dreier, 130
Dreksler, 24
Drescher, 130
Dresher, 19, 20, 159, 164, 165
Dreyer, 159
Drozdowski, 23

E

Edler, 162
Eichenblatt, 129
Eidelberg, 128
Einwohner, 128, 129
Eirelberg, 129
Eisen, 128
Eisenberg, 128
Eisenstein, 128, 129
Elyashev, 14
Epstein, 164
Ettinger, 135
Eydelberg, 112, 115
Eydelsberg, 110, 159
Eydlsberg, 159

F

Fayershteyn, 19, 20, 24
Faygenboym, 60, 109, 114
Faygnboym, 115, 116
Fecher, 24, 27
Fechter, 24, 25, 26
Feigenbaum, 135, 136
Feldman, 112, 135, 136, 161
Fensterbloy, 76
Ferder, 136
Ferger, 136
Feuerstein, 136
Fiechowitz, 44, 45
Fiegler, 135
Fingerhut, 160
Finkel, 136, 161
Finkelshteyn, 19
Finkelstein, 162
Finker, 135, 136
Fischler, 136
Fishler, 24
Fleschler, 135
Fleshler, 24, 160
Flusman, 160
Flussman, 136
Foigelfus, 135
Foyglfus, 42
Friedman, 135
Futerman, 117, 135, 161, 165

G

Garczynski, 126
Gartler, 16, 130, 160
Gelberg, 67
Gerecht, 130
Gerekht, 160
Gershteyn, 159
Gerstein, 130
Gertler, 130
Ginzburg, 53, 56
Gitt, 130
Glatnz-Leyeles,, 68
Gold, 163
Goldberg, 120, 130, 160, 163
Goldman, 130
Goldshteyn, 86
Goodman, 61
Gordon, 163
Gosker, 53
Graetz, 53, 57
Grand, 163

Grass, 130
Grinberg, 53, 57, 97, 163
Grinboym, 15, 17
Grinshteyn, 159
Grinstein, 130
Griss, 154
Grobshtok, 160
Gut, 159

H

Haken, 163
Halberstat, 131
Halpern, 31, 105, 118, 131
Harman, 131
Hartman, 131
Hartshteyn, 24, 159
Hartstein, 131
Hazanovitch, 156, 158
Hefner, 61
Helfman, 131
Helshteyn, 54
Hering, 77
Herring, 131
Hershteyn, 163, 164
Hertman, 131
Hertz, 67, 71, 162, 164
Herzl, 16, 26
Hochman, 131
Hoffman, 131
Hofman, 24, 26, 54
Hokhboym, 159
Hokhman, 164
Holtshacker, 159
Holzfierer, 131
Holzhacker, 131

I

Iwanska, 84

J

Jashlikover, 133

K

Kahane, 156, 158
Kahn, 163
Kaner, 137
Kanner, 141, 161
Karski, 69, 70, 94, 95
Kasche, 137
Kastelanski, 83
Kastelman, 137
Kats, 162
Katz, 111, 118, 133
Kazimierz The Great, 8, 11
Kenobl, 115, 116, 161
Kerpel, 19, 20, 24, 121
Kerpel, 137
Kershenboym, 115
Kesselman, 162
Kestlman, 161
Kirschenbaum, 137
Klepfish, 51
Klog, 86
Knabel, 137
Knobel, 13, 136, 144
Kohn, 60, 61, 63
Kolodnitzki, 137
Koppelman, 136
Kornbrener, 161
Kornbrenner, 137
Kornfeld, 24, 137, 165
Kot, 69, 70
Kramer, 136
Krishtal, 86
Krop, 136, 137
Kuenstler, 136, 137

Memorial Book of the Martyrs of Krasnystaw

Kuni, 164
Kupershtok, 106, 118
Kupperstock, 137
Kutshman, 162

L

Lander, 134, 160
Langman, 110, 133
Laufer, 10
Lebensbaum, 162
Leivik, 70
Lerer, 20
Lerman, 24, 48, 54, 133, 134, 163
Lerner, 24, 133, 160
Lev, 160
Levkovitsh, 54
Levkowitz, 133
Lew, 133
Lewartowski, 156, 158
Leyvik, 69
Liberman, 50
Licht, 133
Lichtenshteyn, 147
Lichtenstein, 162
Lichtstein, 133, 162
Lichtzieher, 133
Likhtenshteyn, 81, 110, 115
Linetski, 53
Listhoyz, 113
Lofer, 53
Lope, 54
Lorber, 50
Lowenstein, 133
Luft, 24, 115, 133, 160
Luftik, 162
Luria, 49
Lusthaus, 133, 134
Lusthoyz, 16, 24

M

Mandeltort, 134
Mandler, 134, 160
Mandltort, 29, 160
Mapu, 18, 22, 53
Mark, 156, 157
Markewitz, 134
Mayman, 48, 54
Maymon, 19, 163
Mehrenstein, 134
Meiman, 134
Melamed, 31, 32, 37, 39
Mernshteyn, 16, 24
Mikołajczyk, 90
Miller, 164
Mirlas, 76
Mitelman, 111, 112
Mitlman, 24
Mittelman, 134
Moycher-Sforim, 22
Mozsitzer, 134
Mushkat, 50
Muterperl, 144, 160, 164
Mutterperl, 134

N

Niedziałkowski, 83, 84
Nirenberg, 134, 160
Nirnberg, 112
Novogrudska, 86
Nowakowski, 69, 70
Nusker, 134

O

Obenshteyn, 159
Ochsenberg, 128
Ohn, 129

Oksenberg, 42, 44, 159
Opazdawer, 129
Orczynski, 69, 70

P

Pecher, 135
Pechter, 20, 135, 136
Pelts, 24
Peltz, 136, 160
Pelz, 136
Perets, 22
Peretz, 7, 10, 11, 53, 129, 149, 154
Perlmuter, 19, 20, 21, 24, 25, 26, 121, 160
Perlmutter, 24, 135
Pinker, 135, 136
Pletzl, 135
Plock, 136
Plotnicka, 158
Polkovnik, 107
Prechter, 18, 19, 20
Prekhter, 160
Prylucki, 8
Pryłucki, 11
Puterman, 141

R

Rabinovich, 22
Raczyński, 91
Raychman, 18, 19, 20, 24
Raykhman, 111, 114, 115, 160, 161
Refoyl, 37, 38, 42, 45
Reichman, 137, 138
Reichstein, 137
Reiss, 137
Rimer, 137
Ringworm, 45
Robinsohn, 137

Roitstein, 137
Rosen, 137
Rosenbaum, 137, 138
Rosenblatt, 137, 138
Rosenblum, 137
Rosensweig, 137
Rozen, 96
Rozenblat, 24, 25, 112, 161
Rozenboym, 74, 111, 114
Rozentsvayg, 24, 45
Roznblum, 163
Rozntsvayg, 160

S

Saltzman, 132
Schack, 138
Schneider, 24, 138
Schneidwasser, 138
Schwarts, 164
Schwarzbier, 138
Sechser, 132
Segalovitch, 68, 70
Seifer, 132
Sharf, 10, 53
Shifer, 60, 61, 62, 63
Shiye, 20, 50
Shloss, 67
Shmaragd, 20, 50, 112
Shneour, 68, 70
Shok, 20, 24, 49, 108, 110, 115, 116, 141, 160, 165
Shtemer, 19, 121, 161
Shtentsl, 68, 70
Shtern, 19, 20, 33, 147
Shteyn, 20, 24, 106, 118
Shtitser, 54

Shtuntsayger, 4, 5, 13, 16, 18, 19, 20, 21, 27, 31, 35, 42, 105, 115, 116, 141, 148, 160, 161, 165
Shtuntsyger, 161
Shulman, 86
Shvarts, 161
Shyuntsayger, 161
Siegelschiffer, 132
Sikorski, 90
Silberlicht, 132
Silberman, 132
Silberreich, 132
Silberzahn, 132
Silverberg, 164
Simon, 163
Singer, 24, 72, 128, 132
Sitzer, 132
Slonimski, 53
Smarand, 138
Smolenskin, 18, 22, 53
Spindel, 138
Stack, 134, 135
Starzyński, 84, 85
Statman, 162, 163
Stein, 138
Stemmer, 138
Stepanski, 114
Stitzer, 138
Stok, 160
Stonzeiger, 138
Stunzeiger, 1

T

Taytlboym, 115
Teitelbaum, 133
Tenenboym, 16
Trager, 132
Tragerman, 132
Trumpeldor, 156, 158
Tsuker, 24, 42, 46
Tsukerman, 47, 48, 53, 54, 60, 97, 145, 146, 163, 164, 165
Turakeltaub, 132
Turger, 133
Turkltoyb, 160

V

Valdman, 16
Valik, 159
Varman, 22, 25, 131, 132, 141, 159, 165
Varshniter, 33
Vaynrib, 159
Vayser, 20, 24, 25, 29
Vaysvasser, 16
Vership, 163
Vizenberg, 31, 110, 113
Vogelfuss, 135

W

Wagner, 132
Waldman, 131
Walik, 131
Wank, 131
Warschgitter, 131
Wegener, 162
Weinberger, 132
Weinrieb, 131
Weinstein, 131
Weiss, 131, 162
Weisserwasser, 131, 132
Weisswasser, 131
Wiesenberg, 131

Y

Yaffe, 156, 158, 164
Yitzchaki, 34, 49
Youngman, 133
Yungman, 21

Z

Zak, 163, 164
Zaltsman, 28, 159, 160, 165
Zaremba, 83, 96
Zayd, 163
Zayfer, 19, 20, 22, 24, 25
Zigelshifer, 144
Zilberaykh, 118
Zilberlicht, 24
Zilberman, 21, 112, 159
Zilbertson, 24, 111
Zinger, 25, 54, 159
Zitser, 22, 24, 26, 159
Zucker, 136
Zuckerman, 4, 6, 10, 136
Zukerman, 5
Zygelboym, 67, 68, 69
Zygielbojm, 34, 35, 70, 71, 72, 74, 76, 77, 78, 79, 80, 82, 85, 86, 87, 88, 89, 90, 91, 92, 93, 94, 95, 96

www.ingramcontent.com/pod-product-compliance
Lightning Source LLC
Chambersburg PA
CBHW051525230426
43668CB00012B/1738